The Unfair Advantage

My Story of Conquering the Beast of Addiction

by John Robert Eddy

The Unfair Advantage
My Story of Conquering the Beast of Addiction

The Unfair Advantage is a work of nonfiction. To protect their privacy, the names of some individuals, places, and institutions have been changed.

This book contains general information about addiction, recovery, and related matters. The information is not medical advice. This book is not an alternative to medical advice from your doctor or other professional healthcare provider.

ISBN: 978-0-578-89202-3

Robby Eddy and *The Unfair Advantage* – WINNER OF THE 2021 BEST INDEPENDENT BOOK AWARD *for* Substance Abuse Recovery Memoir.

To my beautiful wife, Monica,
And our amazing children, J.C., Alina, Peyton, and
Junior

CONTENTS

CHAPTER 1: Locked Up

A man reaps what he sows – Galatians 6:7

I woke up in the tawdry hotel room in the Florida Panhandle under a sense of doom: This was the day I would be locked up. My sheets were sweat-soaked; what little sleep I had managed had been filled with nightmares.

I was scheduled to turn myself in at the United States Federal Penitentiary in Marianna that day, just down the highway. My case had made national headlines: "Florida Man Sentenced for Role in $30 Million Telemarketing Scam."

But the truth is, that crime—the one they had finally been able to make stick—was just the tip of the iceberg. I had done far worse, and with far worse people. I had been arrested forty-five times, including five DUIs. I had almost died a violent death any number of times, once by a contract killing (but the would-be assassin, fortunately for me, had turned government witness). I had riddled my mind and body with powerful drugs and nonstop drinking, living on the very edge of death—in fact, in an ambulance I once found myself *looking down* on my coding body as the paramedics frantically applied the defibrillator paddles.

I forced myself out of the hotel bed and hit my knees on the floor, praying for strength, because the last thing I wanted was to let my poor mother and father know how scared I was.

A knock came on the door and I let my father in. "Do you want to grab some breakfast?" he asked.

I had zero appetite, but I didn't want my dad to know

1

how I was really feeling. He is a very strong man—a retired Army Airborne Recon soldier—and I have always looked up to him. "Sure," I said.

My father, mother, and I got in the black Mountaineer and drove to the Waffle House. I could only force down a few bites. As I sat there in the booth wishing time would slow down, I couldn't help but notice the sadness on my mother's face. She had grown up a "Southern Belle" and was still a lovely lady—it was hard to see what this was doing to her.

The waitress, an older Southern woman, was very sweet. Her cheerful demeanor helped lift my spirits for a moment. My father had told her we were in Marianna to "take care of some wreckage from my son's past." She looked at me and smiled and said, "This too shall pass."

We went out to the Mountaineer and commenced the longest drive of my life, though it was just a few miles— I watched my parents' GPS tick them down. I took out my "burner" phone—I'd had to sell my iPhone to raise money for the prison canteen (yep, even in prison you've got to pay your way)—and saw text messages from some true foxhole buddies, men who had stuck with me in my battle for sobriety over the two preceding years: "You'll be all right—God's got your back." "We'll be writing and visiting." "We'll see you when you get out." The messages were encouraging, but my friends seemed far away right now.

The GPS announced our arrival. As we rolled into the parking lot, I looked up at white, thirty-foot high walls topped with barbed wire all the way around (I would discover three more layers of chain-link fence inside the walls). Gun towers manned by black- and blue-uniformed guards projected above the walls. My heart raced as the reality of my situation came crashing down on me. Due to my extensive criminal history, I was having to turn myself in to a pretty bad prison, one riddled with gangs and "politics" and armed guards. My anxiety only grew as we got out of the Mountaineer and made the long walk to the front entrance.

Inside the double doors, the guards behind the counter looked up and asked us who we were and what we were doing there.

"I'm here to turn myself in," I said.

One of them looked at me like I was crazy, then he looked at his colleague and they both laughed. "Look, buddy," one of them said, "people don't turn themselves in to a United States Federal Penitentiary." I knew what he meant: "self-surrenders" usually presented themselves at county jails.

"My name's John Robert Eddy," I said.

That brought a flash of recognition to one guard's face. He typed my name into the computer, then slowly nodded. "He's serious," he said to the other guard.

Then they got to work on me. They asked for my ID and told me to empty my pockets of all my belongings. I took out my wallet and they told me to empty it. As I did, my Two-Year Sobriety Medallion fell out. At the sight of it, grief and panic rushed over me. Over the past two years, I had finally made a new start in life, and now my past had reached out and clawed me back. I asked if I could use the restroom and they said yes. Barely holding myself together, I crossed the lobby, entered the men's room, and went into a stall, where I fell to my knees for the second time that day. "God, give me the strength to go through this!"

Reentering the lobby, I saw the tears on my parents'

faces. The officer motioned me behind the counter, patted me down, and then handed my belongings to my parents.

"Which gang do you affiliate with?" the officer asked, speaking gruffly now. "I see you have tattoos." His next statement: "Don't worry, you'll fit right in here. You belong to the Feds now."

He pointed to an open cell and told me to go inside it. I looked back and told my parents goodbye one more time; tears ran freely down their cheeks as they held each other.

I walked into the cell, which had no windows, just cold metal benches. Behind me, I heard the heavy steel door slowly sliding closed until with a loud *clink!* it suddenly slammed shut with a shock that shook the cell. Grief and panic rushed over me again.

Oh, God, I'm in prison.

CHAPTER 2: How Did I Get Here?

All the days ordained for me were written in your book before one of them came to be – Psalm 139:16

The guards strip-searched me, dressed me in prison khakis, took my picture for my prison ID, then led me down a hallway to double doors that opened to the courtyard. "Navajo House," they said, pointing to the dorm farthest away. "Follow the sidewalk."

I set off alone.

"Fresh meat!" prisoners actually called out, like a line from some Hollywood movie, as I walked past the laundry room door.

It felt like I was walking inside some medieval castle, with the tall walls all around and the high towers at the corners (the razor-wire chain-link fences inside the walls, however, were thoroughly modern). A guard station stood in the middle of the yard, reflecting my image in its black one-way windows. Manicured grass (cut by the inmates, I would learn) bordered the sidewalks that led to the various buildings.

"Fresh meat, where you from?"

I kept walking.

The sliding metal door of Navajo House opened as I approached, and the guard—or "correction officer" (CO)—let me in. As he took my ID and checked me in, I looked around at my new home. It was a triangular room with two tiers, the upper one ringed by a walkway, upon which prisoners sat, legs dangling over the edge, eyes on me. Other prisoners walked around the room. Still others watched TV. There was a set in each point of the triangle, and the segregation was obvious, with whites watching their TV, blacks their TV, and Latinos their TV. The walls of the dorm were white cement block.

The CO pointed out my cell and I entered it to find two cellmates. One was an older man, sitting on his bunk wearing a black beanie. I would learn that he had been "down" (that is, locked up) for thirty-five years and was doing life. The other cellmate was a Latino gang member, covered body and face with tattoos. They could not have been happy to see me. The cell, only six by eight feet, was hardly large enough for two men; the authorities had somehow sandwiched a third bunk between the other two on the wall. A metal bench anchored to the floor, a desk anchored to the wall, a toilet, and a few small combination lockers made up the rest of the furniture.

"You a chomo?" the Latino said. "I gotta ask."

"What's that?" I said.

"Child molester."

"No!"

"I also gotta ask: You got your paperwork—your 5K1?"

"I just turned myself in from the streets. I don't know what you're talking about."

"Your docket sheets, the history of your case, to prove you didn't testify against no one. Either of those, a chomo or a snitch, you need to check into solitary within twenty-four hours or get stabbed up."

"I'm neither of those," I said, and went back out to the CO to put in a request for my paperwork from my attorney.

Before I knew it, *clangs!* and curses rang out, and I

turned to see two inmates squaring off. Each held a plastic chair in front of him as a shield while his other hand wielded a weapon. One man swung belts tied together and fixed with two combination locks at the end; each time he hit the chair, plastic shards went flying. The other man jabbed away with a twelve-inch shank, a "homemade" weapon he had formed from some piece of overlooked metal. Other prisoners swarmed to the fight, pulling out their own shanks.

As I watched, my own adrenaline surged, and I'm thinking, *Fight or flight?*

My next thought: *How will I ever make it through five years here?*

And I had to wonder: *How did I end up here? When did I cross the line that put me on the path to federal prison?*

"SLD"

I never knew my biological father, but I may have inherited from him more than I liked to believe. He was a thief, among other things, and my mother left him while she was still pregnant with me to move into a double-wide on her parents' property.

My grandparents were both recovering alcoholics, my "Papa" having been sober for over thirty years thanks to a Twelve-Step program. I always remember him with a wad of Red Man in his cheek and a tool in his hand, either under a hood in the driveway or over a piece of wood he was fashioning into some useful article, like the rocking chair he had made for himself. I must have gotten my mechanical abilities from him. I had heard stories about his drinking days—he had been the kind of drunk to wake up shaking violently until he got his first taste—but I never saw him like that. In fact, I never once heard him raise his voice, lose his temper, or curse.

My mother did not escape her parents' drinking years unscathed, however. Bad memories lingered. As a result, my mother and her brother Marty never touched a drop in their lives, but her brother Johnny went the other way and became an alcoholic (though later he got and stayed sober and became a great guy). I have noticed this same phenomenon in the lives of other people who grew up in alcohol-damaged homes, either a desire to stay as far away from that lifestyle as possible or a tendency to slip right into it themselves.

I seemed to have been born with a knack for mischief, according to the stories I've heard. Nanni watched me while my mom was at work, and she let me get away with practically anything. Once while I was still a toddler, I found my way to her gas heater with a book of matches. Luckily, I only burned a big hole in her thick carpet, which she quickly covered with an area rug so no one would know what I did. I would fill my pockets with dog food and run around her house and yard, snacking on it. One day my sister came outside and saw me playing with a twelve-inch butcher knife. That was the last straw; the next day I was enrolled at La Petite Academy.

We lived in Jacksonville Beach, Florida (where I had also been born, in 1982). These were hard times for my mother, who was raising me and my sister Jamie (who was seven years older than me) all alone. Somehow I have very early memories of her sitting on the swing outside, holding me and crying as she watched the buses go by. I could not have been more than two years old.

It was about this time that the man I call my real

father, and my hero, came into our life: John Carroll Eddy. It is no surprise that he became my hero; after all, he was ex-Airborne Recon with the 101st Airborne Division (the Screaming Eagles), a martial arts practitioner, and a boxer. What's more, he had a character that more than matched his military pedigree and physical prowess. He and my mother worked at the same bank. They got to know each other over a couple years' period, fell in love, and more than thirty-five years later are still going strong.

When I was five, we moved down the Florida coast to West Palm Beach, where I would spend all of my school years. When it came to school, I always felt "less than," a step behind. As early as penmanship class in elementary school, I was cheating to get by. To make my letters look like they were supposed to, I placed my paper over the book and traced them. When the teacher fell for that, I traced over some Disney characters and showed them to my dad. He was so impressed he was ready to enroll me in the school of the arts! Often through the years, I copied other people's work to pass. Sometimes I would follow a good student up to the teacher's desk when we were turning in work, sneak his paper away, and erase his name and insert mine. It's crazy to think about those things now, but I see that I had a deceptive streak in my character from an early age, a streak that would go nuclear when drugs and alcohol were added to the mix.

Early on I was labeled SLD, that is, a "Slow Learning Disability" student, a tag that stuck all the way through high school. Really, I just had trouble paying attention and being interested. Nice ladies would come take me out of class to read my tests to me. It made me feel different from everyone else, an outsider. My temper made things worse. I would get frustrated and snap a pencil or toss a desk. So I was given a therapist to see weekly. I think this hurt more than helped me, because it made feel like something was wrong with me.

Another blow to my self-esteem occurred in middle school. I had spent the summer at Nanni's in Jacksonville, and she had fed me (it seemed) fried chicken and biscuits three times a day. I loved it. But when I went back home for middle school, I had put on so much weight that other kids made cracks about it. Now, in addition to the SLD tag, I was a chubby kid.

My dad and football came to the rescue. My dad bought me my first weight set, and I began to work out hard, like I had seen him do, and get in shape. And in football, which I began playing about that time, I found something I was good at, and loved. I remember the first time in practice I got hit really hard. A kid named Jimmy leveled me, leaving me flat on my back and sucking air. Rather than discouraging me, my first thought was, *Hey, I can do the same to him.* And the next play, I did—left him flat on his back. I remember the look of respect he and I exchanged moments later. My dad would say about me, "Robby's as tough as shoe leather and mean as a snake."

My dad always told me that I could have or do anything in the world as long as I dug deep and worked for it. He drove this lesson home one summer when he taught me how to cut down a tree, the huge pine in our yard.

First, he had me get a ladder, climb to the treetop, and loop a rope around the upper trunk. Then I climbed down and Dad took the end of the rope and walked across the road with it, pulling it in the direction he wanted the tree to fall. As he held the rope, I chopped away. After it fell, I cut it into logs, which I carried one by one to the curb.

If I thought the chore was over, I was in for a surprise. Dad brought me a shovel and said, "Now get the stump out."

I spent *hours* digging away at that stump, shoveling around it, trying to get the blade under it, whacking at the roots. It barely budged.

I went inside and said, "Dad, I can't get that stump out. It's impossible."

He looked at me and said, "You know why you can't get that stump out? Because you don't want to bad enough."

That got to me. I went back outside and tore into that stump and roots. Sweat poured off me, my hands blistered and bled, my rib muscles cramped, but I kept digging. Until *finally* that stump plopped out of the ground, and I fell back on the grass with a great sigh of relief. Catching my breath, I turned to the window and saw my father looking out at me, nodding proudly.

Toward the end of eighth grade, I told him that I wanted to be the starting fullback on the high school football team. He said, "Are you going to talk about it or *be* about it?" I told him I was serious.

Some days later, he drove home with his pickup bed filled with old tires. He got out and went into the dirt road that ran by our house and marked out forty yards. Then he had me run the forty yards, timing me. The result was not impressive.

He said, "If you want to be the starting fullback, you're going to have to work at it." He took a tow rope, tied it around my chest, and attached one of the tires to it. "Now run the dash." I did and came back panting. He said, "Practice like that, adding another tire to the tow rope each week."

That's what I did. While other kids were lazing around the house, sunning at the beach, or partying that summer, I was lifting weights in my garage or running down the road like a wild man, six or seven tires tied to me. My forty-yard dash speed at the end of the summer was 4.6, top-notch for a ninth grader. (The first couple times I ran the dash without the tires I fell flat on my face, I was so used to hauling that weight.)

The hard work paid off. I started for the JV team that fall, setting rushing records, and was moved up to the varsity before the season was over.

"Robby! Robby! Robby!"

But even as I entered ninth grade and high school, and had success in football, I still struggled with self-esteem, still found myself in search of an identity. For one thing, the SLD baggage clung to me, as did the chubby kid image, though I had dropped the extra pounds and muscled up over the summer.

One day, in a matter of moments, I found my new identity—or it found me. My friend Chandler and I had just left PE and were entering the crowded lunchroom. Our high school was a big one, with about 3,000 students, so hundreds of kids were there, seated around those long cafeteria tables. Looking around, you could see the usual divisions, the "cool kids" (popular and good-looking) sitting at one table, the "jocks" in their ocean-blue letter jackets at another, the black-garbed "freaks" at their table, and the "rednecks" and "preps" and "nerds" at their various tables.

12

Chandler and I were passing the tables on the way to the serving line when some kid standing there dropped his shoulder and drove it into Chandler. Immediately, I lunged and popped the kid in the face. I had always had a hair-trigger temper and before I knew it I was leaning over the kid, pummeling him.

It just so happened that this took place at the edge of the "cool kids'" table, and one of them, Patrick, climbed up on the table and started chanting my name, "Robby! Robby! Robby!" You see, Patrick was a neighborhood friend; we had worked out together in his garage, heavy metal music pumping along with the iron. (But he sat at the cool kids' table; I did not.)

So as I'm pounding on this poor kid, Patrick is chanting my name, and all of a sudden the whole cafeteria joins in: "Robby! Robby! Robby!" It was amazing to hear my name sweeping like a wave from table to table, and the feeling that came over me was this: *I've arrived.*

And indeed that was the moment when the chubby SLD kid became "the dude you don't want to mess with." My new persona was born, a persona that catapulted my life down a whole new path.

As the school cop and the principal rushed in to separate us, to put us on the school golf cart, and to drive us out of there, I could still hear kids chanting my name.

After my suspension (ten days), when I returned to school, everything had changed. The cool kids talked to me and invited me to parties. Other kids wanted me for a friend. And girls started to pay attention. After dropping those pounds, I was a fairly good-looking kid, with blond hair and green eyes. Plus, I was clean-cut, and my dad had taught me to be a gentleman to girls, opening doors for them and so forth, as well as to respect adults, answering, "Yes, sir," or "No, ma'am." Now the girls were showing interest, and, believe me, it was mutual.

Fighting, sad to say, became a part of my daily life. If someone "had a problem with me," I would fight before school, in school, and after school. I would fight at parties. I had an MO: "Robby will fight." Classmates even *arranged* fights for me. If some guy with a "tough" reputation transferred to our school, someone would egg him on: "Bet you can't take Robby." Eventually, the new kid and I were squaring off at Little Blue Park. Sometimes it seemed like the whole school showed up to watch and cheer me on. Kids even filmed the fights.

All of this was so different from the way I'd been raised. My dad had taught me some of his fighting skills when I was very young, but only so I could defend myself; only so I wouldn't have to walk away from a fight because I was afraid, but could walk away because I was the bigger man. But I had left those high ideals behind.

The odd thing about this negative attention was that it only fueled the desire for more. Like a drug. Like alcohol.

One day after football practice I came into the locker room with the rest of the team to see two words scrawled in black marker across my locker: "Roid Rage." I was so physical on the football field and off it that people assumed I was "juicing." That really bothered me at the time, because I had never touched a steroid, or any other drug (or alcohol) for that matter. My size and strength were the result of hard work and a good diet.

But I remember thinking, *What would happen if I did use steroids? What would they think of me then?*

14

Those two words, "Roid Rage," would prove prophetic in the worst way.

CHAPTER 3: Gateway Drug

Wine is a mocker and beer a brawler; whoever is led astray by them is not wise – Proverbs 20:1

Like everybody else at our high school, I knew Bryce and Russ Owen—or, I knew of them. They were twin brothers whose father was a wealthy contractor in a big housing development near West Palm Beach. Bryce drove a brand-new Chevy Silverado 454 pickup, shiny red, supercharged, and jacked up on 44" Super Swamper tires. Russ drove a yellow souped-up Camaro Z28, also brand-new. They were popular, good-looking, and always had cash to burn.

They also had a well-earned reputation as "bad boys." They built pipe bombs, blew up mailboxes, and even started a large fire in the nearby "woods." Their parents had divorced and their stepfather was a fireman. After starting the fire, they ran home and told him about it, but did not mention that they had started it. When the newspaper printed an article about the fire, they cut it out and saved it like some trophy. I didn't know them at the time (they were a grade ahead of me), but I heard the stories.

I used to see them at Ultima Fitness, the gym where I would work out after school, and I noticed that they had beefed up, become well-built. I remembered how skinny they had been in middle school, no muscle mass at all, so it caught my attention. At the time (my tenth grade year) I was going to Ultima Fitness with my best friend, Victor Flores, because I was helping him train for

16

wrestling.

One day we got to talking about what it would be like if we used steroids. Would it help Victor build muscle (he was kind of little at the time)? Would it help me keep the fat off while making me stronger? We drifted over to where Bryce and Russ were working out, struck up a conversation, and asked, "Do you guys know anyone who can get us steroids?"

"Yeah, *we* can," they said.

They said it would cost about $250 for ten vials, which would last about twenty weeks, a full cycle's worth.

The next day we met Bryce at the gym and made our first purchase of Sustanon 250, which Bryce and Russ had bought in Mexico.

"How do you take it?" we asked.

"You inject it into a muscle with a syringe, the deeper the better. If you're only going to shoot your shoulder, get a 1-inch needle. But for the buttock or leg, a 1.5-inch needle." Clearly, these boys had done their research. "You can get the syringes at the drugstore," he said. "If they ask what you want them for, say it's to paint in the small spaces on model cars."

We went to the drugstore and got the syringes without any questions asked, then drove to Victor's grandparents' house in Loxahatchee. I had butterflies the whole way there. Partly, I was excited about the steroids. Partly, I was worried, a gut feeling telling me this wasn't right. In retrospect, I realize God was warning me through my conscience (the Big Book for Twelve Steppers refers to this voice of warning as the "God-consciousness within"). I tuned it out.

At Victor's grandparents' house, we went into the

bathroom, adrenaline really pumping now. We debated who would go first and somehow decided it would be Victor. I filled a syringe with two cc's from the vial—it was an odorless liquid, the color of cooking oil—and expelled the excess air from the syringe. Victor planted one foot on the floor to support himself and held up his other leg so that the buttock muscle would be loose. I positioned the syringe and planted the needle in the muscle.

"Did it hurt?" I asked, but he just shook his head and smiled—he was as pumped as I was.

Then it was my turn. I planted one foot, held up the other leg, and Victor injected me with the steroid. My heart was pounding so much I barely felt the needle. In fact, I imagined I could already feel the juice working, making me bigger and stronger. (It actually takes about a week for results to show.)

But it wasn't long before the results were apparent. In about eight weeks, I went from 180 very fit pounds to 225 even fitter pounds, all muscle growth. And on the football field and the wrestling mat (I was also a wrestler), I was just killing it.

There *were* side effects, including increased aggression, feelings of invincibility, and heightened sex drive (anabolic steroids are a synthetic form of testosterone, the male sex hormone). But I could handle that stuff (I thought). The improved speed, strength, and size were worth it. I concluded that my conscience had worried me needlessly.

Little did I know that I had opened the door to a very dark path. Many people speak of marijuana as the gateway drug, the one that leads to harder and more dangerous drugs down the road. Mine was steroids.

"It's Not a Drug...."

Victor and I met up with Bryce and Russ several more times over the following months to purchase steroids. They noticed we were building muscle mass. After a while, they asked if we wanted to hang out with them. Did we want to meet up later and go to a keg party? This was sometime the following school year, my junior year.

We met at their house that night. Russ was still getting ready for the party, so Victor and I went in Bryce's room. We couldn't help but notice the stacks of $100 bills on his dresser. More money was visible in an open safe on the floor, as well as packs of steroids. I could see that selling steroids was lucrative, to say the least.

"Are you going to drink tonight?" Bryce asked me.

"No. I'm working hard towards a football scholarship. I don't want to risk it."

"What about 'scoops'? You heard of that?"

I shook my head.

"GHB," he said, and pointed to some water jugs on the floor, each filled with a slightly brown liquid.

"Never heard of it, but I don't do drugs."

"It's not a drug," Bryce said. "Body builders use it. It used to be sold in GNC stores."

"Really?"

Bryce went on to say that GHB released natural growth hormones and burned body fat. "One small cap will not only give you a buzz, but burn fat." That was music to my ears, what with my insecurities about my weight and my desire to build my physique.

I know now that GHB is one of the *worst* drugs out there. In fact, one of its slang names is Grievous Bodily Harm (other nicknames include G, Liquid Ecstasy, etc.).

19

It is a common "club drug" and "date rape" drug. GHB actually contains chemicals commonly found in floor stripping solvents and drain cleaners!

But at the time I didn't know any better, and what Bryce said about it burning fat and helping muscle growth was quickly changing my mind about GHB.

Right about then the doorbell rang and a few moments later Patrick walked in the room—the same Patrick who had jumped up on the cafeteria table and chanted my name. He was carrying a water bottle, and after saying hi, he unscrewed the cap on his bottle, handed it to Bryce, and asked for some "G." I watched as Bryce poured the fluid from one of the jugs into the cap, then poured the cap into the Patrick's water bottle. He did this eight times, which, I would learn, amounts to two ounces' worth.

"Are you going to take some, Robby?" Patrick asked me.

Patrick being a good friend, it eased my fears to see him enthusiastic about "G." So when Bryce suggested we all take a capful, I went along. It tasted awful, like saltwater times a thousand. But moments later the buzz came, a euphoric feeling, a warm rush flowing through my entire body and up to my head. My steroid use had made me cocky, but this stuff was way more intense. I felt ready to take on anyone or anything, literally.

"Let's go to the party," Bryce said.

We all piled into his Silverado 454, the "Red Beast," and drove to Tim and Karen Warren's house. There were dozens of cars parked outside. When we walked up and rang the doorbell, Tim answered, saw the twins, and shook his head. "I can't let you in," he said. "I was told, 'By no means Bryce and Russ.'" As I mentioned earlier, everybody knew the twins' reputation. I was starting to get a similar one, with all my fighting and cockiness and growing size.

"Ah, come on, Tim," we said. We could see the house filled with kids partying and listening to music.

"Can't do it," Tim said and shut the door.

Bryce and Russ gave each other this look, and you could tell these twins could read each others' minds and were about to wreak some havoc.

"Go grab them out of the truck," Bryce said.

Russ stalked to the truck to grab whatever "them" was, but Bryce walked straight over to the driveway, where the Warrens' cars were parked, right in front of the garage. He pulled his shirt off, wrapped it around his arm, then busted the driver's side window open. He reached through the window, found the garage door opener clipped to the visor, and pressed it. The garage door opened.

I just stood there watching in amazement, hyped up on the GHB.

Bryce entered the garage, took a fire extinguisher off the wall, then walked to the door leading into the house. He threw the door open and let loose with the fire extinguisher, hitting kids in the face with the white foam and spraying the inside of the house.

I looked to see what Russ was doing. He had taken what looked like large firecrackers from the truck (I learned later that these were quarter sticks of dynamite!) and was lighting them one by one and inserting them in the tail pipes of the cars.

By now there was complete pandemonium. Girls screaming, kids running out of the house to escape the fire extinguisher, only to be greeted by the *bang! bang!*

bang! of dynamite sticks exploding in metal tail pipes.

"Let's go! Let's go! Let's go!" Bryce yelled, tossing the fire extinguisher aside. "Hurry up, Russ!"

We ran to the Silverado, jumped in, and hauled it out of there. The windows were down, the sunroof open, and we were all yelling with excitement, adrenaline pumping. Bryce put on "Mudshovel" by Staind and as the music blared rocked back and forth in his seat. I got to know this rocking mannerism very well in the coming years; both he and Russ did it when they had just broken the law or were about to. I developed that same rock.

"Let's go to the Boo!" Russ said.

Boo was the nickname for Peekaboo, an eighteen and older strip club. We weren't old enough, but Bryce and Russ said they knew the bouncer there and could get us in....

... And so was set the pattern of my life for the rest of high school, a weekday routine of football practice, working out, and injecting steroids, followed by a weekend of GHB use, partying, and seeing what mischief Bryce and Russ had in mind.

It usually involved crashing some kegger. Folks at these parties would know trouble had arrived when the Red Beast rolled up and four muscle-bound dudes climbed out. Lots of these parties were in "the abandoned house" in the woods across from Okeeheelee Park. Huge parties, with lines and lines of cars parked along the roads. We'd always down a capful of G before getting out. Walking past the cars, Bryce and Russ would pick up rocks and hurl them at the windows; Victor and I followed suit. We'd walk through the partyers, pick up the keg (even as kids were trying to fill up their Red Solo cups), and carry it off. If anyone said anything to us, we'd rough them up. One time we fired frozen paint balls at the partyers before hauling off the keg. The strange thing is, we often didn't even drink from the keg we stole; in fact, I never did, still avoiding every drop of alcohol in hopes of a football scholarship. We just wanted the adrenaline rush.

One time we picked the wrong party, deep in Loxahatchee where we didn't know a lot of people, and ended up surrounded by a bunch of skinheads—bare-chested dudes in combat boots and red suspenders. We held our own in a brutal street fight with them, in which both my eyes bloodied, but eventually they would have overwhelmed us—had not the approach of a dozen police cars sent everyone scattering, including us.

End of a Dream

Toward the end of my senior year, I got the bad news: Dana College in Nebraska, a Division II school, would offer me only a seventy-five percent scholarship to play football for them. My parents would have to come up with the rest of the money, which couldn't be done.

It was devastating news: My football days were over.

The truth of the matter is, you have to be extremely gifted to go far in football. I was talented and tough, but not anywhere approaching pro-level abilities. And in spite of my weightlifting and cheating with steroids, I wasn't big enough for that level of competition. It wouldn't have made sense for my family to hawk their entire future to send me to Nebraska to play football.

Still, everything I had worked for all those years had come to nothing. I was sad and depressed, my self-esteem shot.

Plus, I had no idea what I was going to do after high school—football was my only plan! Other kids were going to college to earn a degree. Some were going into the military. Some had jobs. Nothing but uncertainty lay ahead of me.

I *was* looking forward to graduation, however, happy that I was actually getting to walk with my class. Our graduation was held at a big auditorium in Fort Lauderdale, with about 700 of us in the class of 2000 all dressed up in ocean-blue gowns and caps. My parents, sister, and grandmother came to support me (my grandfather had been killed by a drunk driver some years earlier). The truth is, I was mostly looking forward to the celebration *after* graduation, going out and getting "messed up." In fact, Victor and I had already started the "pregame," tossing back a capful of GHB even before the graduation ceremony began.

When it was over, we asked all the kids where the parties were and followed a bunch of them out to Singer Island (named after an heir of the Singer Sewing Machine family), where kids from various schools had rented rooms in a resort on the beach, to party door to door in the hotel. Victor and I joined them and in one room met a guy from another school who was drinking a clear liquid from a glass jar, one of those preserves jars with a metal lid.

"What is that?" I asked him.

"Moonshine," he said.

I laughed because I thought that was only in the movies. But he was serious; it was homemade liquor. He handed me the jar and, without a thought, I took my first-ever drink of alcohol. I downed it like it was soda!

Almost before I knew it, I was truly "messed up."

GHB and alcohol, both depressants, are a dangerous mix. At some point, I passed out. I woke up later on the floor, the party still raging. I got up and drank some more.

Meeting some girls, we drifted out to the pool, where some people were rolling a blunt, which is marijuana packed inside a cigar wrap. They offered it to me and, just like with the alcohol earlier, without a thought I smoked my first weed. They say marijuana is a mild, safe drug, but it blew me away; in some ways I found its effect on my mind more potent than GHB and alcohol.

So there I was—dawn had not cracked on the first day of my post-graduation life—and I had added alcohol and weed to the GHB and steroids flowing through my system.

I couldn't get any higher or drunker, I would tell myself in the following days, thinking about graduation night. But the crazy thing is, I would certainly try. In fact, in the days and years to come, it would seem as if I was living with an unquenchable thirst for more—booze, drugs, thrills—a thirst I would go to unthinkable lengths (as you will see) to satisfy. I have since learned that no amount of alcohol or drugs or money—or anything else—can fill that void in us, nothing but a Higher Power. As the famous quote by St. Augustine puts it: "You have made us for yourself, O Lord, and our hearts are restless until they rest in you."

But I was some years and many heartaches away from learning that lesson.

CHAPTER 4: Rise and Fall

Like a city whose walls are broken through is a person who lacks self-control – Proverbs 25:28

After graduation, I felt lower than I ever had. High school was over and my college football dreams had come to nothing, and I had no idea what I was going to do. But my dad had always taught me a good work ethic (I had held various jobs since I was thirteen, cutting lawns, clerking at stores, etc.), so I didn't just laze around after high school ended but hit the pavement looking for work. About all I had to offer, however, was a warm body, so the best I could find was a "buggy buster" position at Walmart, rolling the carts from the parking lot to the store. I did meet a cute girl there, blond-haired and blue-eyed Ashley, who looked like she belonged in some fashion boutique rather than behind a cash register at Walmart.

One night about eight I took my break, sitting outside on one of the benches in my Walmart vest. When I got up and went back inside, the moment I stepped through the double doors, this guy, about five-foot-three and stocky, came walking toward me with a look of rage on his face. Before I knew it, there was a knife in his hand, and he swung it at me, a wide lateral stroke as though to cut me in half at the waist. Instinctively, I managed to dodge it and at the same moment brought an overhand right down on his jaw. His knees buckled, the knife fell to the floor, then he fell beside it. He wasn't "out," so I continued to pound him, my steroid-ignited aggression flashing full-flame. Plus, I'm furious, thinking, *This guy*

26

tried to kill me!

By now everyone came running—cops, managers, fellow employees—and broke it up. The senior manager declared that I had to be fired on the spot, but a cashier spoke up, a woman I didn't know. She said, "He didn't do anything. That guy attacked him with a knife."

Well, that cashier's comment saved my job—and more. In fact, it led to one of the biggest breaks of my life, an "out of the blue" blessing (and one, sadly, I would quickly squander). When I came into work the next day, Craig Burton, the loss prevention manager, called me into his office. "I saw what you did last night." He looked closely at me. He was clean-cut with glasses, shirt, and tie, and wore cowboy boots. "I was impressed. How would you like a job with me?"

"Really?"

"Walmart has a rigorous loss prevention program. We prosecute everybody. And if they try to run, you can take them down." (Those were different times!) "Plus, there's a raise."

Needless to say, I took the job—and loved it from day one! I got handcuff-certified by the sheriff's department. I developed my own "stealth mode" tactics, such as climbing a ladder in one aisle to look down at a potential shoplifter in another aisle. I ditched the dorky vest for a "wife-beater" T-shirt, baggy pants, and a ballcap worn backwards—and got busy breaking records. The most shoplifters ever nabbed at this Walmart in one month had been seven. In my first month I caught thirty; in my second month, forty; in my third month, twenty-five. I made a sport of it, sometimes even concealing myself in a rack of clothes to see someone slip an article inside their coat; track them to the exit; and, once all points of purchase were passed, move in for the bust. And if they tried to run—well, good luck to them! I chased them down, tackled them, and slapped the cuffs on. Other Walmart employees made a game of watching me, wondering who I might catch that night and how.

Mr. Burton said that if I kept up the good work, I could one day be in his place, making over $100,000 a year, traveling around to the other Walmarts and basically being the boss of guys like me.

Everything had turned around for me, "out of the blue."

You're probably wondering *why* that guy attacked me with a knife, like I certainly was at the time. Well, it turned out that Ashley, that cute blond cashier I was dating, had a boyfriend the whole time—the guy with the knife. I had no idea about him, but apparently he found out about me, and came for blood.

I started dating a new girl, Megan, whose mom worked in the same Walmart in the sporting goods department. Megan and I were pretty close, and I hung out at her house quite a bit, and couldn't help but notice a wide array of brand-new appliances and electronics equipment in the house. Which surprised me, since Megan's mom was single and, like I said, working at Walmart. It began to dawn on me that, night after night, Megan would show up at Walmart about the time her mom was getting off work and proceed to walk me around the store with her. One night, when Megan was leading me up and down the aisles, I told her I had to go back to the office for some paperwork. Instead, I headed for the sporting goods department, slipped behind a shelf, and saw Megan's mom standing alone there with a grocery cart full of merchandise. As I watched, she pulled Walmart bags out of her purse and stuffed the items in the cart into the bags. Then she pulled out some old receipt and headed for the front of the store.

I followed, at a distance. Knowing what was coming, I was partly heartbroken, because this was my girlfriend's mom, and partly mad, because they had both used me. I waited until she rolled past the points of purchase, through the lobby, and into the parking lot.

Then I went out after her. "Laura!"

She stopped and turned.

"Laura, you're going to have to come back in the store with me, and you know why."

Her eyes got big as saucers and her jaw dropped.

I took hold of the cart and waited for her to lead the way back inside.

She was prosecuted and fired.

After this incident, I was truly the Golden Boy at Walmart as far as loss prevention was concerned. I had proven how seriously I took my position. "I really appreciate your work," Mr. Burton said. "You're meant for this job."

First DUI

After graduation, I had nothing in hand, and nothing to look forward to. Now, in just a few short weeks, everything had turned around for me. I had a good job, which I loved and excelled at. I had a promising career ahead of me. I had the respect of my coworkers, and I felt good about myself. All of this just "out of the blue." The headline over my life should have read, "Clear sailing ahead."

But lurking in the shadows of my life, just out of sight

but always stalking, was a cunning and powerful foe: addiction. Just biding its time, waiting for the right moment to strike. Now the blows came one upon another.

The first blow came in the little town of Clewiston, Florida, about an hour from my home. I had been sent to "clean up" a Walmart in that area, where theft was rampant. One weekend some friends and I decided to hang out there in a hotel and have a good time. Victor was there (I'd gotten him a job at Walmart) and so was Jeffrey, my original trainer at the Palm Beach Walmart, a six-foot-four bruiser with shaved head and goatee. We had been playing drinking games when someone said, "Let's go get cigarettes."

I volunteered to drive since I had just gotten a brand-new Chevy S-10 pickup. We piled in, Jeffrey in the passenger seat holding a bottle of Jack Daniels, Victor in the back seat with a twelve-pack on his lap. We weren't on the road five minutes before blue and red lights flashed in my mirror.

My heart dropped. I pulled over and went through my first field sobriety test—all the stuff you see on TV, walking the line, finger to nose, etc. Needless to say, I failed. I was taken into custody and booked in the Hendry County Jail, where I spent eight long hours before being bonded out. (The day would come when I would dream of an eight-hour stint.)

This was my first DUI. My license was suspended. My boss—Mr. Burton—heard about the arrest and was disappointed with me. And my self-esteem took a serious hit. "Out of the blue," I had been given a great opportunity for a lucrative career at Walmart, doing a job I loved, and I was jeopardizing it!

"Well, Well, Well. Which One Are You?"

The second blow was another arrest, this time for multiple offenses. I was hanging out with Bryce and Russ one night in their nice two-story house (it was a model home their contractor father had built, where they were living temporarily) when they suggested we go to a strip club. Jackie Clarke, Russ's girlfriend, was right there with us, and she got mad, of course, but that didn't stop Russ. The strip club they had in mind was a twenty-one and older club, and this time when I told Bryce and Russ I wasn't old enough, they said they'd help me make a fake ID. I gave them my driver's license; they used a pencil eraser to remove the "82" from my date of birth; then they glued new little black numbers (bought at an office store) in their place. "That will get you in."

I looked at the ID. It wasn't a faultless forgery, but I guessed it would get me past a strip club bouncer.

I was to learn the hard way that altering my ID was a bad idea. The law stated that if you tried to pass off someone else's ID as your own, that was a misdemeanor. But if you altered your own ID, like we just did, that was a felony.

When we pulled into the club parking lot, I got out, put my Michelob on top of the truck, then saw a friend of mine in the parking lot. "Juan!" I said. "What's up, bro?" Juan and I had gone to high school together, and he also worked at Walmart. Suddenly, I saw a well-built guy with a back-facing cap walk up and grab Juan. Immediately, I moved in to help Juan, throwing the well-built guy on the ground—from which he frowned up at me, pulled a chain necklace out of his shirt, and showed me the badge on the end of it.

I couldn't believe it: I had just thrown an undercover cop on the ground.

Of course, when he got up, I was now the focus of his attention. As he went through my wallet, he found two IDs, the altered one that said I was twenty-one and a legit one that said I was eighteen. "Well, well, well," he said. "Which one are you?"

He arrested me for underage drinking and possession of a fake ID. Off I went to another eight-hour stint in jail. My second arrest in as many months.

My boss at Walmart got wind of this arrest too, but he still didn't fire me. Mr. Burton always seemed willing to believe in me. But I was losing faith in myself, depressed about what I was doing to my life. But I didn't stop drinking and doing drugs, because that was about the only time I didn't feel bad about myself. That's the deceptive power of alcoholism, the disease that assures you that you don't have a disease.

Home for Thanksgiving?

Another blow fell at Thanksgiving. On the day before Thanksgiving, my dad said to me, "Son, tomorrow is Thanksgiving. Your grandmother is going to be here. Can you please make sure you're here too?" I remember feeling kind of aggravated at that question, thinking, *Of course I'll be there for Thanksgiving and Grandmother. Why wouldn't I be?* But I guess my dad saw that my drinking was getting out of hand.

What he said stuck with me, and so when I went to my buddy Leo's that night, I turned down the beer he offered me, though I wanted it *bad*. "I need to be at Thanksgiving tomorrow with my parents," I said.

He jokingly called me a few names, as if to say,

"Come on, man, don't be a wuss." Then he said, "Just have a couple and go home."

I gave in, but I didn't stop at a couple. In fact, at some point I blacked out, and the rest of the night I can only remember in fragments.... I remember finding myself in some bathroom in some bar, and I'm snorting cocaine off the back of the toilet, my first use of coke.... I see myself popping a Xanax tablet and washing it down with more alcohol.... Then I'm coming to in front of Leo's, sitting in the driver's seat, and he's telling me I better stay at his place, but I tell him I have to go home.... Then I'm braking at a stoplight at the intersection of Royal Palm and Okeechobee Boulevards, about 4:30 a.m. while it's still dark out.... I black out and the next thing I know it's daylight and cars are rushing by and a police officer is banging on my window—I'm still sitting at the light at Royal Palm and Okeechobee!

"How much have you had to drink?" the officer asked.

"Nothing," I said.

He pointed at the Corona in my lap.

When he searched my truck, he found marijuana in the ashtray. "Whose is this?" he asked.

"That's not mine," I said, and, ironically, it actually wasn't.

"Yeah, sure," he said.

So I had another multiple-charge arrest, for "driving under the influence" and for possession of marijuana. This time I was in jail for twenty-four hours before getting bonded out. Of course, I didn't make Thanksgiving with my family and grandmother.

Now—in a matter of months since my first drink—I had been arrested three times, including two DUIs. As I tell people in Twelve-Step programs or prison groups, when I put booze, or any other mind- or mood-altering substance in my system, lawlessness pumps through my veins. I turn into a real Dr. Jekyll and Mr. Hyde.

Addiction and Detox

In the midst of all this, my work numbers started to slip. I'd gone from catching thirty shoplifters a month to three or four. I was using GHB daily; in fact, every two or three hours I'd exit the store and go to my truck for a "scoop."

My Burton called me into his office. "I know something is wrong, Robby. Your numbers are down, and these DUIs and arrests you're getting—if corporate gets word…." He shook his head. "I don't know what it is, but something has to change."

I left his office that day knowing my job was hanging by a thread. I decided on the spot that I would quit GHB. *That's it. I'm done.* But as I walked around the store and the hours passed, including the hour I would have normally gone out to my truck for a scoop, I started to shake, sweat, and feel an uncontrollable anxiety. My heart raced, my stomach cramped, I felt dizzy. Even my teeth tingled. I had one overwhelming thought: *I must have a scoop!*

It was a scary moment, a sneak-peek at what addiction was all about.

I exited the store, slipped into my truck, and grabbed the "water" bottle from the cupholder. I opened it, poured a capful of GHB, and drank it. Within a minute, goosepimply warmth flowed from my head to my feet; the relief was wonderful.

But as great as I suddenly felt, I was also scared to

death, because now I knew I was addicted to GHB.

It was a real wakeup call. And one I actually listened to in the following days.

I went to Mr. Burton and asked for a week off to get myself together. I didn't tell him exactly what was going on, but I think he kind of knew. Then I went to my parents and told them everything—about the steroid use, the GHB, etc.—and they very lovingly let me settle on their couch to detox.

The next few days were a nightmare. The withdrawal symptoms I had experienced in the store multiplied, intensified. My blood pressure spiked, my body ached. I couldn't sleep. I started to hallucinate. I was so racked with pain that at one point I grabbed my dad's red wine and chugged it. Then his Wild Turkey. Only to end up drunk and detoxing at the same time, a horrible feeling. In a desperate attempt to sleep, I went to the medicine cabinet and downed half a bottle of Nyquil. Then I went outside to smoke, and hallucinated even more, imagining that the bushes were coming to life. Literally, a nightmare....

But somehow, slowly, the pain eased, the withdrawal symptoms lessened, and I found myself being freed from the grip of GHB. At least as far as a physical addiction was concerned. My heart and mind had not changed, as you will see.

Grand Theft

Though I had beaten the GHB (for now), my drinking increased. In fact, within the year I would be arrested four more times for underage drinking. I would continue to walk around free, however, because they didn't take you to jail for those busts but gave you a "written arrest," which is a notice to appear in court on a certain date (where I got community service). Still, five underage drinking arrests in one year! You might think I would sit up and take notice, tell myself, *There's another problem to address.* Instead, all I thought was, *You have to stop getting arrested.* Alcoholism is incredibly deceptive.

Only about a month after my detox I was over at Bryce and Russ's place one night, and Bryce said, "Robby, you don't have a problem. Just take the GHB normally."

My first thought was, *No way!* I'd just gone through that nightmare of a detox. I'd have to be crazy to start doing it again.

"You haven't done it in a while, Robby," Bryce said. "Go ahead."

Would you believe it? That is all the argument it took to persuade me. I took a scoop.

You might find it incredible that after all the ruin this drug had worked in my life, and after that miserable detox, I would so quickly, with so little resistance, toss back a capful. I share your amazement. But I have since learned that selective amnesia is common to addicts, who have trouble remembering, as our Twelve-Step program puts it, "the suffering and humiliation of even a week or a month ago."

Plus, those open court cases were hanging over my head. My self-esteem was on the ocean floor. And I was getting to the point where I no longer felt comfortable in my own skin when sober. The GHB seemed to make sense.

I took the scoop, the warmth flowed through me, and in moments I felt on top of the world. What court cases? What problems?

"Let's go have some fun," the twins said.

We climbed in Russ's new truck, a big blue Ford F350 Dually, and drove out to Wellington's polo fields and equestrian clubs area. This is a wealthy community with big houses on huge properties with barns and horses. I didn't yet realize what we were driving out there to do, which was to look for four-wheelers to steal. About midnight we spotted an ATV in an open barn. We drove off a ways to park, got out, and snuck up to the barn. (Russ's girlfriend Jackie was with us; she stayed with the truck as our getaway driver.)

"The keys are in it!" Bryce whispered as we approached the ATV.

We rolled it out of the barn without turning it on, to keep from making any noise. When we were far enough away from the house, Russ turned the key, we climbed on, and we raced back to the truck and Jackie, our adrenaline pumping. We lifted it onto the bed of the truck.

"There's another one next door," Russ said. "Let's go grab that one too."

We ran back and saw another ATV in an open barn. The people in this house had their windows open and were inside watching TV. We crept into the barn. This ATV did not have the keys in it, but Russ knew what to do. He pulled off the ignition cover, tied two wires together, and the engine roared to life. We hopped on and drove back to the truck, our blood roaring with GHB and steroids.

Obviously, there was no room on the truck for another ATV, so Russ drove it out of there, the rest of us following in the truck, all the way to the woods outside the Lion Country Safari park. We hid the ATVs there next to a sleek gray Porsche 911, which Bryce and Russ informed me they had stolen the night before. In the following days, we changed the VIN numbers on the ATVs—a process Bryce and Russ taught me—and ordered a new ignition for the second one we had stolen. (In those days, ATVs didn't have titles, so all you had to do was call a dealer, say you'd lost your key, give the make and model, and they'd send you a whole new ignition and key in the mail.) We advertised the four-wheelers in a trade paper and sold them for the full price.

We started pulling these capers night after night. And we didn't stop with four-wheelers, but took boats, Jet Skis, and (from houses under construction) ACs. Soon I was walking around with thousands of dollars in my wallet, and I'm not yet twenty. I burned through it fast, though, supporting my drug habits and blowing the rest in clubs and bars.

I had crossed another line in the process: I was now a full-fledged thief, completely foreign to my upbringing. Like I said, when I put drugs or alcohol in my system, larceny flowed through my veins.

One night, back in Bryce and Russ's kitchen after stealing four-wheelers, we were "chopping it up"—i.e., talking over everything we'd been doing—when they looked at me and said, "Robby, you're undercover security at Walmart. You hold the keys to the kingdom. You control the cameras, alarms, everything. You could walk out of there with anything you want."

This was back in the day when PlayStation and Xbox were taking off. We could make a killing selling that stuff. We sat there in the kitchen and made up our "Christmas list."

The next night at Walmart I roped my friend Victor into helping me (he also worked in security at the store). We sat in the loss prevention office, where fifteen to twenty screens monitored all the activity in the store. We waited until about an hour before closing and then shut off the cameras in the back stockroom. We went back there and began carrying game consoles, portable DVD players, DVDs, and CDs out into the alley. When work was over, we drove back there, put the stuff in the truck, and then took it to Bryce and Russ. They would pay us on the spot, $1,000 to $1,500 per night.

About a week or two went by, until one day I came into work and thought Jeffrey was acting kind of strange, the way he followed me and Victor around. Plus, I noticed four or five loss prevention managers from around the district in the store, obvious in their shirts and ties.

"Why are those guys here?" I asked Jeffrey.

"Oh, just some routine work."

I shrugged. I was too high to suspect that anything was up, or to care much.

I got a call on my walkie-talkie to come back to the office. As soon as I walked back there and walked through the door, my heart fell in my shoes, because I recognized the setup. Two of the loss prevention managers sat side by side in chairs, with an empty chair across from them. They pointed to the empty chair and said, "Take a seat." They were there to interrogate me! One to ask the questions, one to be a witness. I had sat in their chairs many times, grilling some poor shoplifter. Now it was my turn!

But I said, "No way, man. I'm out of here!" I turned and walked out the door.

Immediately I heard the sound of keys jingling and walkie-talkies screeching, and I knew that sound: cops running through the store! I had called them in many times. I quickly ran back in the office.

The cops rushed through the door after me, looked at the managers with some confusion, then said, "Robby, who is it? Who you got?"

The managers shook their heads. "Robby doesn't have anyone. We've got Robby."

The cops looked at me with shock and disappointment.

"And we got his coworker in the other office," the manager said.

Shaking their heads, the cops moved toward me, but I said, "Hold on! Hold on! I'll talk, but I don't want no cops around."

The managers nodded. "Okay. Can you officers give us a few minutes?"

The cops stepped outside the office and closed the door.

"We were always afraid of someone like you going bad, Robby," one of the managers said. "Because when they do, knowing what they know, it's *real* bad. And that's what it's been with you."

The other manager nodded.

"Listen. You're not in any trouble yet. Just sign here, stating that you took all this stuff, and we won't press charges. You'll just have to pay the money back over time."

I could have laughed, because I had used that same line with many shoplifters. It was complete baloney. As soon they signed, even if they only admitted to stealing a pack of gum, we charged and prosecuted them.

"And we know what you have in your pocket."

He meant the bottle of GHB, of course, stuffed in the left pocket of my cargo pants. At the time I didn't know how they could know about it, but later I learned that Jeffrey had planted a pinhole camera in the office, rigged to turn on when the other cameras went off. What that hidden camera had caught would not have been enough to pin a grand theft conviction on us, however, because it would not have shown us taking the merchandise out of the store. That's why they needed me to sign that confession.

I pulled the bottle of GHB out of my pocket, poured it in the garbage can, then threw the bottle in after it. I cursed them and said, "I'm not telling you guys nothing."

They called the cops in, who tossed me against the wall and handcuffed me. They put Victor in cuffs too and began to lead us out of the store. I'll never forget that long walk. Customers stared, but the most humiliating part was walking past my coworkers, the very same people who had once cheered me for busting others. It was one of the lowest feelings in the world, even high on GHB.

They searched my truck and found a bunch of steroids, so by the time they finished charging me—at the Hendry County Jail again, where I'd gone for my first DUI—I faced charges of possession of schedule one steroids, possession of schedule one GHB, petty theft, and grand theft. (They didn't charge Victor with all that. I think they knew I was the one behind it all.)

This time my bond was serious: $100,000, which meant my parents would have to put down $10,000 to get me out pending trial. The crazy thing is, they did it. Looking back, I think I had entangled them in a typical state of parental codependency, and they probably softened my fall way too long.

But it was only because of their amazing love for me—a love that would be tested more than they could imagine.

CHAPTER 5: A Bottom

I sink in the miry depths, where there is no foothold
– Psalm 69:2

The weeks following my arrest at Walmart were miserable. I had let everyone down. Serious charges hung over my head. And I had thrown away my future.

I spent a lot of time going back and forth between courts in Palm Beach County and Hendry County. In the process, I received another "out of the blue" blessing: Somehow or another, all my charges from the Walmart arrest were dropped—the grand theft, the possession of schedule one drugs, and so on. To this day, I don't know what happened. My guess would be that my original loss prevention manager, Craig Burton (who hired me), and my original trainer, Jeffrey, put in a good word for me. Those two guys always cared about me and saw the best in me (what I could be without drugs or alcohol in my system). However it came about, all those charges disappeared, leaving only the two DUI charges to face.

I went before Judge Sicklen in the Palm Beach County Courthouse to face them. He was a short guy with white hair and glasses, whose nickname was Judge *Strict*land, because he had a reputation for toughness. This first time before him, however, he treated me fairly leniently, agreeing with the state prosecutor to offer me ninety days in a halfway house or ninety days in jail, plus one year of probation. I chose the halfway house—a no-brainer.

The Fern House

The name of the place was the Fern House. It was located in an older part of the city by a big mobile home park and next to small industrial shops. It had one large building, which housed fifty men, six to a room, and a smaller building, a chapel. This place would play a very important role in my life over the next three years: I would be court-ordered there twelve times (and never stay sober) and go there once on my own (and stay sober). I'll never forget the sign that was posted on the wall outside the chapel entrance:

When the Pain of Remaining the Same
Becomes Greater Than the Pain of Changing
We Will Change

I was a model citizen my whole ninety-day sentence at the house, working a job during the day (ironically enough at Greater Yamaha, an ATV shop), getting back to the house by 6:00 p.m. each night, attending all the Twelve-Step meetings, and not touching a drop of alcohol or GHB (of course, there was none on the premises).

But most of what I heard at the place went in one ear and out the other. I did not believe I was an alcoholic. For example, one weekend when my parents visited, they said to me, "Robby, you can't drink or do drugs anymore."

"I just have a problem with drugs not alcohol," I said. "What about when I get married and there's champagne—you mean to tell me I can't have a glass with my wife?" I could not envision a life without alcohol.

Whenever anyone "graduated" from the Fern House, they had a big farewell meeting, all the men gathering around to wish you well and say goodbye. At mine, the house manager—a big black dude named Bernard—took me aside and said, "Eddy, you're gonna be back, man. You're not done." Bernard had been a hardcore user on the streets, a real "garbage can" (someone who takes or tries anything), but he had completely changed. He could see that I had not. I had simply been "dry" the last ninety days—without booze or drugs. I had not become "sober"—without booze or drugs *due to a purposeful program of recovery.*

As soon as I walked out of the door that ninetieth night, I went to my truck, called my friends, and was on my way to a keg party in minutes. But as I drove, I thought about the things I'd learned at Fern House, what Bernard had said, and how I'd been ninety days without booze or drugs. It kind of scared me to rush off to this party and start right up drinking again. I wanted to test myself to see if I was an alcoholic or not, so when I got to the party and everybody was shoving beers and drinks at me, I turned them all down. Man, was that *hard,* because I would have loved some.

But I made it through, and I woke up the next morning thinking, *Wow, I did it. I knew I wasn't an alcoholic.* I didn't understand yet that it's not so much the first drink that makes an alcoholic, but what comes after the first drink: an uncontrollable desire for more, regardless of the consequences. That same day I went out with some friends to Peanut Island and on the boat ride there was offered a Corona. I hesitated, thinking again about ninety days of sobriety, but then remembered: *Look how I said no last night. I'm not an alcoholic.* I took the beer, took a drink, and can't tell you today how many more I had that day—because I ended up blacked out. I had not been able to stop once I started.

A couple weeks later I hooked up with Bryce again and again started doing GHB. Right away, I was doing that stuff all night long, hanging out at strip clubs, and all the rest. Just as if I'd never quit.

That's another thing about alcoholism and drug addiction: They're progressive diseases, they don't retreat. Sober ninety days or ninety months, it doesn't matter. Pick up the bottle again, take the drug again, and you're right where you left off.

That's where I found myself.

Back to Jail

I had kept my job at Greater Yamaha, but now that I was back on GHB all day my work ethic began to fade, to say the least. The owner would catch me nodding off at my desk, because GHB not only makes you soar, it makes you sleepy. One day he sent me to work the front register, and the idea suddenly popped into my head to open the cash register and take some money—I pulled out about $400 in fifty-dollar bills. The crazy part is, there was a camera right on me! I didn't care; I didn't think twice. The next day, back in the stock room, I got the idea to steal Go-Peds—those little motorized stand-up scooters—so I tossed them over the fence to collect later. The day after that I was back at the register again and this time took $250. Like I said, booze or drugs in my system, larceny in my veins!

That night (the same night I took the $250) I saw in the store a sticker advertising Pit-Bull Stands, a brand of motorcycle stand. On the sticker was a cool image of a pit bull. I stole that sticker, drove to Ink Link Tattoos, and told them to ink that image of the pit bull on my arm. I paid for the tattoo with the $250 I'd stolen.

Suddenly, I was crazy hungry—GHB does that to you too—so I got in my truck, drove to Albertsons, walked down one of the aisles, and ripped open a package of ham on the spot and started eating it. I had every intention of paying for it, but I was so high and so starving I couldn't wait. A manager walked up, backed by four associates, and asked what I was doing. The associates were young guys, so I felt threatened and immediately snapped. I started throwing things around, pulling items off the shelf, even punching myself—steroids mixed with GHB! I cussed them, walked right out of the store, and climbed in my truck.

I pulled out onto the road, and the next thing I knew a cop car was pulling up behind me, lights flashing.

This time—my tenth time, if you're counting—I was arrested for shoplifting and driving on a suspended license. But this time there was no chance of getting bonded out, because I was still on probation—my year was not up.

In the meantime, Greater Yamaha had finally watched their cash register film. Here I caught another break, because the owner—a really good guy, and himself a recovering alcoholic—did not press charges. And they had recovered the Go-Peds I'd thrown over the fence. I learned all this from my poor dad, who had gone in to speak to him. "Robby was doing great," the owner had told him. "A hard worker. We were happy to have him. Then he completely changed." Dr. Jekyll and Mr. Hyde.

As I sat in jail waiting for my court appearance, I began to detox, and it was a hard fall—the sweats, anxiety attacks, sleeplessness. And as my head cleared and reality kicked in, remorse and horror rained down on me.

I went before Judge Sicklen again, and he was not pleased. "Are you kidding me? You just did ninety days at the Fern House, you've been out only three weeks, and you've violated probation with another charge. You're going to the Drug Farm."

The Drug Farm was a stockade in the County Jail, where they dressed you in military boots, made you run every day, and put you through intense drug therapy. Though it no longer exists, it was a pretty good program. It gave inmates facing sentences of twenty or thirty years a second chance; instead, they could go to the Drug Farm for a short track of seven months or a long track of fifteen months. Needless to say, no one facing decades in jail would turn that deal down. But my charges, by comparison, were relatively minor. I didn't think I deserved seven to fifteen months at the Drug Farm, so I denied it.

Here Judge Sicklen lived up to his reputation. "Okay, we'll reset your court date for thirty days so you can think about it."

So back to jail I went.

Thirty days later I appeared before Judge Sicklen again and again denied the Drug Farm. He said, "This time we'll reset your court date for ninety days. Come back then and tell me what you think, Mr. Eddy."

So back to jail I went.

Ninety days later I went back to court and—good news for me—Judge Sicklen had retired. The new judge said, "I'll tell you what. I'll give you another chance at the Fern House, but this time you're going there for six months."

Bernard drove out, picked me up, and took me straight back to the Fern House with him. His words had proven true: I was back.

But this time I was no model citizen. I *did* find a job, at an AC company called Comprehensive AC, but one day, a few weeks in, I lied about going to work and instead called Bryce and said, "Let's do some GHB." He said he was out of the stuff, but he knew where we could get some. I went to his house, got in his truck, and he drove us to—of all places—an Albertsons.

"What are we doing here?"

"You'll see," he said.

We went inside and walked down one of the aisles, and all I could think was, *Did he hide some GHB in the grocery store?* He stopped and grabbed a few packages of super glue remover.

"What's that for?"

"Just hold on. Calm down."

We paid for the packages and exited the store. When we got back in his truck, he handed me one of the packages and said, "Read the back of it. See that—GLB? That's one of the main chemicals in GHB!"

He opened one of the packages. "Take some."

"You're crazy," I said. "I'm not taking super glue remover."

He proceeded to squeeze out a very small amount— much less than a "scoop" of GHB—put it in his mouth, and chased it down with a soda.

I was scared, but I really wanted some GHB, so I followed his example. And would you believe it? Almost immediately, my head got wonderfully warm and then I'm floating. "This stuff *is* GHB," I said, and I was excited about it.

Swallowing super glue remover.

It's amazing the depths to which an addict will sink to get his fix.

Needless to say, I didn't make it back to Fern House. After we got back to Bryce's place, I got in my truck (which I was operating on a suspended license) and started driving up the Florida coast, stopping at every Albertsons along the way to buy super glue remover. I'm not sure what I was thinking, I was so high. I just knew that the phenomenon of craving had kicked in as soon as that chemical hit my system, and I just had to have all the super glue remover I could.

I finally ran out of gas about ten o'clock that night in a little place called Yeehaw Junction—yep, that's its name—and sat in my truck on the side of the road in a real "G-hole"—a trance-like state a heavy GHB user can fall into, sort of like swimming around in a murky, inescapable well.

I managed to call my dad, told him some crazy lie as to why I was out of gas in Yeehaw Junction ("My employer sent me out here on a job," I said!), and he drove all the way out to get me. Then he drove me all the way back to the Fern House, where Bernard and his assistant Clancy were waiting in the parking lot with a drug test. Bernard just rolled his eyes at my excuses and handed me a urine cup. The crazy thing is, I passed the test! That's because the test didn't screen for super glue remover. Bernard and Clancy *knew* I was high—I could hardly speak coherently—but they had no choice but to send me to bed. "We'll figure it out in the morning."

In the morning they called everyone, all fifty guys, into the chapel, showed them a handful of open super glue remover packages—they had searched my vehicle in the night—and Bernard began his speech: "Super! Glue! Remover! I'm an old-school, off-the-street, garbage-can junkie, and I've never heard of anything like this! Pack your stuff, Eddy, and put it out on the breezeway—you're out of here." That was the way at Fern House: If you were caught using, you were publicly called out and sent packing.

I gathered my stuff, walked out to the parking lot, and got in my truck. It was one of the worst moments of my life. I couldn't go home, I was kicked out of Fern House, and now there was going to be a warrant out for my arrest. I was depressed and scared.

I still had my job at Comprehensive AC, so I drove there (on my suspended license). I had a buddy there named Grant, who said I could stay at his place. He used drugs "recreationally," but nothing like me. He warned me, "Robby, you better calm down or you're gonna die." The sad thing is, years later he got heavily into painkillers and ended up dying of an overdose, as did his brother. Addiction is a dangerous monster.

Only a few days after I'd been kicked out of Fern House, while on an AC call at a customer's house, I went into the bathroom and passed out—I was OD'ing on the super glue remover. When they found me, my boss told Grant to take me home. Instead of his place, however, I convinced him to take me to my parents' house. On the way, I got worse and worse, and Grant told me later that I tried to jump out of the vehicle on I-95! I was completely incoherent—"fishing out"— by the time we

51

got to my parents' house. The police came and so did an ambulance. They put me in the ambulance, which (after backing over my parents' mailbox) took me to Palms West Hospital.

When I came to, I had a catheter in me and tubes all over my body, including down my throat. One hand was cuffed to the bed. My mom was there, her eyes swollen and her makeup smeared from crying. She had her hands on my chest and said, "Robby, you're killing yourself. And you're killing me and your father." She told me he was outside on his knees, crying and praying to God: "Please don't punish my son for the things I've done wrong in my life." This was the misery I was putting them through.

Later, my mom, dad, and the police were there, and the doctor came in and told them that I had been digesting super glue remover. Then he poured some of it in a Styrofoam cup and the stuff ate right through the bottom of the cup. The doctor looked at me and said, "You're going to die if you keep it up."

They pulled the curtains shut and stepped outside to talk—the doctor, my parents, and the police. When they did, I noticed the package of super glue remover the doctor had left on top of the heart monitor. Believe it or not, I immediately reached up and snatched it, hid it in my underwear under the hospital gown, and as soon as they took me upstairs to my own room, I found a way to get up, wheel my IV unit into the bathroom, and take it.

Back to Jail – Again

As soon as they medically cleared me, the police came to take me directly to jail for violating probation. They escorted me out of the hospital with my hands

52

cuffed and people watching, through the front entrance, and into the back seat of the police car.

I stayed about sixty days on this stint. I remember calling my mom and dad on the jail phone and saying, "I'm through with drugs and drinking forever. You don't need to worry anymore. I promise you." And you know what? I meant it. If you had given me a lie detector test at that moment, I would have passed it.

The day came when the guard called out, "John Robert Eddy, pack it up all the way." My time was up. I'd been locked up a total of six or seven months now and couldn't wait to get out, this time with no probation hanging over me. Grant and his cousin Connie (who would become my girlfriend) picked me up. Connie drove her green Ford Explorer, I sat in the passenger seat, and Grant in the backseat. The jail was hardly out of the rearview mirror when Grant tapped me on my shoulder, showed me a little blue pill in his hand, and said, "Take this."

"What is it?"

"Lorcet. A painkiller—hydrocodone. It'll help you relax."

I had been dry for weeks and weeks, being locked up. I had told my mom and dad repeatedly, and in all sincerity, that I was done with booze and drugs forever. And yet when I saw that little blue pill in Grant's hand, I took it. I didn't think twice.

How could I have been so sincere about my plans to stay sober and so quickly forget them? It just shows how deceptive addiction is. I had good intentions, but deep down I had not had the "psychic change" that Twelve-Steppers refer to. As the Big Book puts it, I was still "without defense against the first drink" or drug.

So I took the pill without a second thought—and was introduced to opiates.

My head got warm and fuzzy. I felt great and stayed high the rest of the day. When I went to bed that night, I felt like I was floating on the mattress.

I developed a habit pretty quickly. Connie had an aunt named Leah, a crooked nurse who would get us prescriptions for the pills, as well as prescriptions for morphine lollipops and morphine patches. By the time I was working for a new AC company, I was "eating painkillers" all day. I remember how horrible it felt to hear the pills rattle in my pocket, knowing I was running out one by one. What would I do when they were gone? It was an expensive habit, so I reverted to stealing trailers and four-wheelers at night, and on the job I rummaged through customers' cabinets for meds, money, anything.

I had become such an addict that even Bryce and Russ didn't want to hang out with me. Plus, though they had by no means become Boy Scouts, they were both making legitimate money at the time. Russ had started a company that installed hurricane shutters on his dad's new home builds, four or five a week. Bryce was going to school to be a general contractor and take over his dad's business. But one night they showed up, and guess what? Bryce had GHB—the real stuff, not super glue remover. So then I started using GHB again, and I was drinking most nights until I blacked out.

GHB. Painkillers. Morphine. Booze.

Could it get any worse?

One night I was out in the Wellington area again, with the polo fields and equestrian clubs (where I'd first stolen ATVs with Bryce and Russ), and somehow ended up at a high-end apartment complex, and in this older, well-to-do couple's apartment. Suddenly, the lady brought out a pipe and a whitish chunky substance, which turned out to be crack cocaine. She and her husband began to smoke it. I remembered all the horrible things I'd heard about this drug—how it was the most addictive form of cocaine, how it blew up your health, how you did crazy things to get it. But here was this classy couple smoking it, so I supposed it couldn't be that bad. When they offered me some, I smoked it.

I was up all night smoking that crazy stuff.

"I Need Help"

One way or another, I ended up outside the apartment very early in the morning, while it was still dark. I remember staring up at the sky and thinking, *I've got a pocket full of pills, a pocket full of GHB, and now I'm smoking crack. I've got serious problems. I need help.*

I called my dad. He could tell that I was crying. He told me to come to the house.

When I got there, I said, "Dad, please help me. I don't know what to do."

He grabbed me, hugged me tight. "Let's go to the Fern House," he said.

I packed some clothes, called Bernard in tears, and he said, "Come on in."

When we reached the Fern House parking lot, and I got out and was walking to the door, I noticed again that sign posted on the wall by the chapel entrance:

When the Pain of Remaining the Same
Becomes Greater Than the Pain of Changing
We Will Change

This time it hit me like a ton of bricks. I knew exactly what it meant now. I was ready to change!

CHAPTER 6: Something Missing

"They will do such things because they have not known the Father or me" – John 16:3

I was ready to change.

I was hardly twenty-one, but beat-up and tired of the way I was living. It was different this time, checking into the Fern House on my own. I soaked up all the meetings, worked hard through the Twelve Steps (I thought), did all they asked.

I got a sponsor first thing. A sponsor is someone who has walked the road to sobriety ahead of you, who comes alongside to answer questions and help you through the Twelve Steps. Mine was a big, blond, blue-eyed Puerto Rican—Luis Rivera. We met once a week at his house to go through the Twelve Steps. I had actually known Luis prior: His wife was the crooked nurse, Leah!

I also got a job first thing (a Fern House requirement), taking the Palm Tran bus to a big AC company called Air-Ref. They hired me as an installer. I actually consider my walking into Air-Ref that day a Divine Appointment, one of the many times God "had my back" and was looking out for me long before I knew it. The owner, Chris Ryan, was real good to me, even putting me through AC school. I don't think I would be where I am today, a successful AC contractor, without him.

I really shined at Air-Ref, getting moved into my own service truck almost immediately, but there was a "little" problem: I had lied about my driver's license. It had been suspended, but I said I had one. I told myself it was no big deal. *After all, I have to drive to work and go to meetings. God would want me to.* But this "little" bit of crookedness would snowball on me. Lies lead to more lies. And it was a sign that I had not really surrendered all, that I was not really all-in when it came to sobriety, for a number of the Twelve Steps call for transparency and honesty.

I graduated from the Fern House after six months, completing the program. Everyone was proud of me, my mom and dad, Bernard—everyone. Things were going great. I was killing it at Air-Ref. I got my first apartment. I bought a van and started doing some side work in air-conditioning, sometimes making as much on the weekend as I did all week at work. And I was in a hardcore sponsorship group, guys who took staying sober very seriously.

But it seemed like something was missing for me. I'd hear guys in our meetings talk about the "God-consciousness" in their hearts, but it seemed like mine just hurt. There were times after a service call that I would just pull over, feeling anxious and fearful and not knowing why. Looking back, I realize it was because I wasn't all-in. I was supposedly living the Twelve Steps while driving around all day breaking the law—no license, no tags, no insurance. I was "tightening nine screws out of ten," and that's not how this sobriety thing works. It's all or nothing, black or white. At some point the wheels were going to come off.

Steroids?

I started to work out again, hitting the gym, pumping iron, watching what I ate. But it was so *hard* without steroids, mentally and physically, and the progress so slow. Imagine you've been driving a souped-up

Mustang—nitrous-fed, supercharged—and suddenly the extra power is stripped away. It's still a tough car but nothing like before. That's how my body felt without steroids.

One time I was working out with my sponsor Luis, who had a weight set in his backyard, and I asked him what he thought about steroids. "I don't think they're a drug, Robby. I think they just make us better and stronger." I couldn't believe my ears. I was *sure* steroids were a drug, in fact, my gateway drug. But here my sponsor was saying they were okay. Maybe I could try them again? I told Luis I knew where I could get some. He said to get some for him too.

Looking back, I realize this was terrible advice from my sponsor (sponsors aren't perfect). But I don't blame Luis for what was about to happen. I knew in my heart steroids were a drug. Luis just happened to tell me what I wanted to hear at the time.

I bought the steroids from Bryce and Russ, and I'll never forget how I felt the moment I put that needle back in my flesh. It seemed I could literally feel evil start to seep back into me, the devil himself. Immediately my pride puffed up, as I focused more and more on my muscling-up body. And, of course, larceny kicked in: I rented some rims for my truck, then sold that truck with the rented rims on them to raise the price. The company called looking for the rims, but they never got them back from me.

I was going on two years of sobriety (if you don't count the steroids) when I was driving to a meeting one night and the familiar blue and red lights flashed in my mirror. The cop had noticed my expired tags. After I pulled over, he quickly found out about my suspended license. I had Cole, one of the guys in our sponsorship, in the truck with me. I said to the cop, "Come on, give me a break. We're going to a Twelve Step meeting. That's my copy of the Big Book on the seat there. We're working on staying sober." It's funny to think back on, how I was trying to convince that cop I was such a good guy right in the middle of getting caught breaking the law.

The officer wasn't buying it. He arrested me for driving on a suspended license and no tags, walked me to his back seat, and put me in it. Cole got loud with the officer when he saw him put me in the back seat, and he got arrested too!

The arrest should have served as a warning to me and brought me back to the straight and narrow. But the spirit of lawlessness was already gaining prominence in me, and I shrugged it off. I was only glad that I didn't have any probation hanging over my head and was able to get released on OR (my own recognizance), promising to show up at all court dates.

At the "Barbershop"

There's a saying in sobriety circles: "If you hang out at the barbershop, you're eventually going to get your hair cut." Of course, it's a warning to Twelve-Steppers to avoid old drinking and drugging buddies and places. But after buying the steroids from them, I had begun to hang around with Bryce and Russ again. One night we were at a bar—and believe it or not, I wasn't drinking—when we ran into Russ's old girlfriend Jackie, the one who had been our getaway driver for the ATV thefts.

Now I had had a crush on Jackie, who was blond and

green-eyed, since I was about fourteen, but she had never given me the time of day. But now I'm twenty-two years old, all muscular from the juicing and lifting, tan, and feeling confident, and she gave me one look, her eyes got big, and she said, "Robby! You sure grew up!" Of course, that made me feel good (but I could tell it made Russ jealous and mad; the twins didn't like taking second place to anyone, especially when it came to a girl).

But Jackie was hot on my trail. Somehow she got my phone number and started texting me, I texted her back, and she called me over to look at her air-conditioner.... Long story short, we started dating.

I thought I had hit the jackpot. I had *always* liked this girl. But when I told my sponsorship group about her, they shook their heads. "This girl's a mistake for you, Robby," Luis said. "She's from your drinking days, and she's still drinking."

"I know, but I don't have to." I was irritated with them for not being happy for me.

"I know you've been through the Twelve Steps," Luis said, "but you know what they say: It's always money or women that draws a guy back out before he's ready."

We went back and forth about this for a period of time until I actually began to think that these guys who had saved my life were just jealous of me! In reality, they were just trying to save my life again. But I said, "I'm out of here," and left the group.

When Jackie heard, she backed my decision. "You can stay sober without them," she said. "You don't need all that."

"Teach Me How to Sell Drugs!"

Jackie asked me to move in with her, and we ended up going out to Singer Island to live with her dad, who had a house that backed up on the water and a view of Peanut Island. Her dad (Michael) was a big-time coke dealer; he'd been selling cocaine since he was fourteen or fifteen, and he was about fifty now. He was the real deal; I'd once seen him buy a Hummer with cash. He was also a ghost; that is, he kept nothing in his name, not bank accounts, not cars.... He stashed his cash, or invested it in guns, knives, old swords, and antiques, stuff he stored all around the house. He was a doomsday prepper too, very paranoid. You can imagine the way Jackie was raised.

I was fascinated with his lifestyle: the money, the adrenaline rush, breaking the law. One night we were sitting on his couch; he was smoking weed (I had turned it down); and I got the bright idea of asking him to teach me to sell drugs!

"No, Robby, you don't want to do this. It's a rough life." He told me that he had had one job when he was a teenager, busting his tail at a restaurant making five dollars an hour, and he had decided on the spot that he would never work that hard again for mere pennies, and so became a drug dealer overnight. But you could see, if only by the paranoid lifestyle, that it had taken its toll, and he didn't want that for me. I think down deep he had a good heart, but it was buried beneath all those years of drug use and drug selling.

But I persisted. I really wanted to learn how to sell coke! And he said okay.

A week or so later I was in his Cadillac on the way to a cocaine buy. "Just be quiet," he said. "Let me talk." We were going to see his "plug," i.e., his main drug supplier, an MS-13 (or Mexican Mafia) guy. Michael had been doing business with him for years. We drove to a low-income neighborhood north of Miami, pulled up in front of a little house, and were shown into the garage, which had been converted into a den with TVs, couches, a desk, an AC wall-unit. Seven or eight stone-faced Latino guys awaited us, guns in their belts, shaved heads, garish tattoos. Their leader greeted Michael, said, "What's up?" to me, and then the coke and Michael's cash were on the desk. The exchange was made and we were out of there. I found the whole thing a rush, scary but crazy.

Then Michael showed me how to crush the cocaine until it was fine enough to flow through a sifter; then how to "cut" it with a look-alike substance to increase the amount we could sell (the "cut" was bought at a drug paraphernalia shop in a strip mall); then how to "re-rock" it, using a bearing press to compact it back into a hard substance, about the size and feel of a hockey puck; and finally how to break that "puck" into "eight balls," eighth-of-an-ounce pieces ready to sell.

I started selling them right away, to friends, to former classmates, to people in bars and clubs. I built a clientele fast, raking in the money. Overnight I had become a drug dealer.

Relapse

Believe it or not, I was still "sober." Anyway, I had not picked up a drink. But it was only a matter of time. You see, the disease of alcoholism, of addiction, is a patient and subtle foe. It was more than willing to let me drift along, patting myself on the back, telling myself I was doing well just because I had not tipped back a glass—while all the while every crooked step I took was one step nearer its trap.

It would only take one drink.

Strangely enough, it was my girlfriend and best friend who got me to take it. Victor was home from the Marines, and he called me one night wanting to hang out. He came out to the house on Singer Island, and he said, "Wow, Robby. You really got your life together, man." He saw the money, how I was ripped from the weights and juice, and how I'd ended up with Jackie, the girl of my dreams. Of course, I ate it up, acting all cool and bigtime.

He and Jackie were drinking beers, and they kept asking me to have one. "Robby, you're one of the most disciplined people I've ever met in my life," Jackie said. "You can have one drink and just go back to your sobriety tomorrow. It's no big deal."

"Please, man," Victor said. "I haven't seen you in years. Have a beer with me."

And here the disease of alcoholism sprang its trap. I had gotten so far away from the Twelve Steps, from my sponsorship group, and from any sense of God, that all my defenses were down, and I suddenly conveniently forgot my own track record, the ruin and misery that *always* accompanied drinking in my life.

"Yes," I said. "Fine. Just tonight."

I took the beer, took the drink—and didn't stop. The phenomenon of craving triggered and I couldn't get enough.

I drank beer after beer and then I thought, *I've been selling this coke and I don't even know if it's any good.*

"Maybe we should try some of my coke?" I had two bags with me, one with the cut cocaine, one with the pure cocaine. I took out some of the good stuff for me, Jackie, and Victor, and once we started, it was on. I can't even remember how much we snorted that night. All I remember is that Victor eventually went home, and Jackie and I kept at it. Then another idea:

"Why don't I cook some of this coke?" Next thing I knew I was at the stove with baking soda and cocaine and teaching myself on the fly how to cook crack. It was Jackie's first time to use crack. We stayed up the next two days smoking it, until all my coke was gone.

Needless to say, I had relapsed.

The terror was back.

The next six or seven years would make my first twenty-two look like child's play.

CHAPTER 7: Beast Awakened

"Sin is crouching at your door; it desires to have you" – Genesis 4:6

In no time at all, maybe about a week, I was shooting heroin into my veins in a Holiday Inn in Jupiter, Florida.

Alcoholism and addiction, like I've told you, are progressive diseases. They had not retreated during my two years of sobriety, but had crouched like a beast in the shadows, waiting for me to have that first beer with Jackie and Victor. Then they roared to life, taking up just where they left off. So it's no shocker that I moved from beer to coke to crack to heroin within the week. I had awakened the beast.

I was actually doing more than heroin in that hotel room. I was "speedballing," which is using cocaine and heroin at the same time. It is highly dangerous (Google the list of celebrities who have died from it) because the stimulant in cocaine and the depressant in heroin— though producing a powerful rush—counteract each other, masking how intoxicated you really are. So it's easy to overdose.

I ended up in that hotel room doing heroin because Cole, one of the men in my sponsorship group—the one who had been arrested with me on our way to the Twelve-Step meeting—called me up and asked, "Do you want to get high?" You see, Cole had never really been "all-in" when it came to sobriety; like me, he had been one of those "tightening nine screws out of ten" guys. When he heard I had relapsed, he called me up and asked

66

if I wanted to get high. I said yes, and brought my cocaine to the party while he brought his heroin.

We started off cooking my coke and smoking crack. I had no intention of doing heroin, but as he brought out his needles and shot up, he looked at me and said, "Do you want some?" He was a young guy, about my age with freckles and red hair, but he had been a hardcore street junkie. "I'll shoot you up," he offered, because I had never done it before.

I remember back at the Fern House how I used to tune out when guys like Cole talked about shooting heroin, thinking, *I would never do that. Those guys are junkies.* But as I sat there considering his question, I noticed that he had a brand-new bag of needles. Believe it or not, that was all the green light I needed to say, "Why not? Go ahead."

Just like that, I became a heroin addict.

Addicted to Heroin

I hadn't told Jackie where I was, or even that I would be gone, so when I got home from Jupiter a couple days later, she was of course really mad and flipping out. I made up some lie (already you couldn't believe anything that came out of my mouth) and managed to keep my heroin use secret from her. In spite of her dad's business, or maybe because of it, Jackie was actually very antidrug.

Right away, the very next day, I was driving around getting heroin from Cole or wherever I could find it. Like I said, I had become addicted to heroin the moment I took it in the hotel room. I started using it every day, and I went downhill fast. I would literally wake up in the morning and begin to have withdrawals. The first thing

I would do is sneak off to the bathroom with my needle and spoon and shoot up before going to work.

Needless to say, my work suffered. I was doing my AC business and installing hurricane shutters on new home builds for Bryce and Russ's dad. I thought I could work high, but after a couple of hours on the job, I'd have to shoot up again. Then I'd nod off. Then I'd wake up and have to shoot up again. Sometimes I couldn't manage to get shutters on a single house. But I would still turn the invoice in to get paid, because my habit was expensive: about $1,000 a week. Making matters worse, I was buying my heroin from a dishonest dealer (what a surprise!), who cut the stuff I bought from him a little more each time, so I had to keep buying more and more to get high.

After six or eight months, I was strung out. Everything was falling apart, my work, my relationships, my finances, even my body. I got so constipated at one point that I had to resort to drastic measures to even have a bowel movement. By now, I wanted off the heroin, but I knew the detox would be so bad, and I'd be so sick…. I didn't want to go through it.

Then one day Jackie went into my truck for some reason and found a brand-new box of needles. She came in the house screaming for me and banged through the bathroom door just as I was putting a needle in my arm. You can imagine how upset she was. She was crying and yelling at me, saying we were through. She got in the truck and drove off, calling a bunch of people, including my mom and dad, telling them how bad I was.

She came back, and I asked her to give me one more chance. I told her about a drug I'd heard of, called Suboxone, that supposedly got people off heroin without withdrawals. It sounded like a miracle drug, and I wanted to try it. I called up a doctor who would put me on it—in Fort Lauderdale—and made an appointment for the next day. The doctor's office told me not to use heroin for fifteen hours before coming in, which was going to make for a *hard* night.

I drank like crazy to make it through that night, along with taking Xanax and smoking weed (which I hated), but the withdrawal pains still hit; my system was screaming for heroin. My dad came to pick me up in the morning to take me to the appointment, bringing a cup of coffee and a bag of McDonald's—my poor dad had no idea how bad I really was. We set out in his Mountaineer. It was about eighty degrees out. I was sweating, shaking, crapping my pants, and throwing up. My dad would have to pull over so I could open the door and dry-heave. My bones ached, my body ached, and I shook uncontrollably. It was about an hour's drive to Fort Lauderdale, but it seemed to take forever.

When we got there, they gave me the papers to fill out, asked for my ID, and guess what? I had forgotten it! My poor dad had to drive me all the way back to my place to get it, with me cold turkey detoxing all the way. When we got there, guess what? Jackie had gone somewhere and taken my wallet with her! No ID. My dad finally decided we better just go to the DMV and get a new one made. Which we did, and the photo showed a bone-thin, sunken-cheeked addict.

Eventually, we made it back to the doctor's office. I lay down on an exam table in a patient's room, and they brought me a little orange tablet to put under my tongue and let dissolve. A little bit later, because I had been doing so much heroin, they brought me a second one.

After fifteen or twenty minutes, the craziest thing happened: The withdrawal pains stopped completely. Just disappeared. Maybe this was a miracle drug? I stood up and walked out of there like it never happened. My dad couldn't believe it either. We went out and got in his Mountaineer, laughing.

Little did I know at the time that I was just replacing one drug with another. Suboxone is a complicated drug, but in essence it works by simulating a dose of heroin to the opioid receptors in your brain, therefore relieving the withdrawal symptoms. Suboxone is itself a partial opioid. It also has an ingredient that blocks the "high" from further opioid use, so why shoot up any more? In other words, it takes away the motivation.

It sounds great: Take a pill or two a day and you're off heroin.

But for me, it was just one drug replacing another. Suboxone gave me a sense and appearance of sobriety without a real inner change taking place. I looked good on the outside. I wasn't strung out. I could work. I was making lots of money in air-conditioning and shutters. But I hadn't changed, deep down.

Within a month, I would be taking steroids again....

CHAPTER 8: It Was All Very Sad

What benefit did you reap at that time from the things you are now ashamed of? Those things result in death! – Romans 6:21

About six months after I got off the heroin, Jackie and I moved up to Port St. Lucie. I had been installing hurricane shutters up there for Bryce and Russ's dad on a regular basis—about an hour's drive each way every day—so we decided we ought to just move up there and find a house. I also thought a geographical change might be good for me, help me stay away from drugs and out of trouble. The crazy part is, I was *already* on drugs, taking the Suboxone pills every day and using steroids. But I had myself and everybody else fooled.

We bought a nice three-bedroom, two-bath house and moved on up there. A couple months later, Jackie had her friend Ellen over, and we decided to have "a few drinks." This was my first drink since getting off heroin—about eight months—but the moment that alcohol touched my lips, the "beast" awakened once more. Before you knew it, we were loaded and pulling out some of Jackie's dad's cocaine to add to the mix. We stayed up drinking and drugging all night, during which Jackie's friend was hitting on me and I was flirting right back. All my morals fly right out the window when I'm drinking or drugging.

About five or so in the morning, when we were coming down from the cocaine, out of the blue my phone rang.

"Who's that?" Jackie snapped, because neither of us

trusted the other (with good reason).

"I don't know," I said.

She grabbed my phone, answered it, exchanged words with the caller, then snapped it shut—it was one of the early cell phones—and threw it at my face!

I found out later it was some guy who called, who said, "Tell your man to stop calling my woman!" Now the crazy thing is, I had no idea who this guy was and I had never called his wife. It was a wrong number! Sometimes I wonder, because of what happened next, if the devil himself arranged that call.

Because I snapped when Jackie threw the phone at me. I dodged it, then grabbed her feet and pulled her off the bed, banging her head on the floor. Her friend tried to stop me, but I pushed her away. Jackie jumped up and ran outside, and I ran after her. Of course, all this time we were screaming and yelling and so neighbors had come out of their doors—it was daylight by now—to see what was going on. They were calling 911 too; I know, because later the prosecutors played the tape for me and I could hear myself yelling in the background.

I caught Jackie, threw her over my shoulder, and carried her back in the house kicking and screaming. I looked out the door at the staring neighbors, yelled, "Mind your own business!" and slammed the door.

Then I heard her friend calling 911!

I decided I better get out of there. I went out and jumped in my truck and drove down to West Palm Beach for the day. When I calmed down, I called Jackie, and she said she forgave me and missed me. But it was a trick. Little did I know that she and her friend were just waiting until I pulled up to the house to call 911. When I walked in, her friend made some smart remark about me being on my way to jail, and I knew they had called the police. Immediately, I grabbed my case of steroids and ran to the woods beside our house to hide it.

On my way back to the house, I heard engines revving and turned to see three or four black-and-white's racing up the street toward me. I stopped where I was, on the driveway. The cops pulled up, jumped out, and drew their guns.

"Get on the ground!"

I knelt on the driveway with my hands behind my back. They grabbed and cuffed me.

"Don't make a move or I'll shoot you!" one of them said.

Meanwhile Jackie and Ellen came outside to watch, Ellen saying, "He has steroids too! He just went and hid them in the woods."

Next thing I knew I was in the back of a cop car and being driven away. I was coming down from the drugs and alcohol and the old remorse and horror were coming on strong. I didn't even know what I was being arrested for yet, but I knew it wasn't going to be good. They took me to the St. Lucie County jail this time, known as "Rock Road" after the name of the street it is on, and booked me on four charges: kidnapping, false imprisonment (because I had carried Jackie back into the house against her will), domestic violence, and possession of steroids.

Like I said, I knew it wasn't going to be good.

Thirty Years of Selling Drugs

Rock Road was one of the worst county jails in Florida. Packed with gang members, there were fights every night. They would lock us down for twenty-three

73

hours (because of the fights), let us out for one hour of rec, and in that one hour there would still be fights. Located in Fort Pierce, the county seat—a more rural area than West Palm Beach or Miami—it was an old jail, and the cops and judges were old school too. They'd throw the book at you for the littlest offense. I met one guy in there who had been locked up almost a year for one small bag of weed.

I had to stay in there six months, even though Jackie tried to get the charges dropped. When I got out, it was Jackie who picked me up, and we stayed together. We had a very sick relationship; she was sick, and so was I, but we felt like we needed each other. Codependents.

After I got out, I *knew* I didn't want to get locked up again. So, though I upped my steroid use and my Suboxone intake, I stayed away from hardcore drugs and drinking. Jackie also stopped drinking, except for the occasional binge, when she would drive down to West Palm Beach to visit her dad. She became my helper at work, putting in the shutters, and for the most part we just worked hard, came home and watched TV, and went to sleep.

Speaking of her father, Michael, he wasn't doing well. Thirty years of selling drugs was weighing on him—he used to talk to me about it—and he was battling depression. His wife, Jackie's mom, had died from a drug overdose some years back. Jackie's brother was in prison, as he had been off and on since he was fifteen. And Jackie was a mess. I think he blamed himself for all this—and he was right! But how could he quit? He was so used to the money, and he didn't have any other work experience or skills.

One day, when Jackie and I were driving around West

Palm Beach, we happened to stop in to see him. We found him naked under his desk and acting crazy, zoned out. We saw open pill bottles all over the counter and realized he was trying to kill himself. We called 911 and luckily got him to the hospital in time for them to pump his stomach and maybe save his life. When it was time for him to get out—after a mandatory 72-hour suicide watch at a behavioral health center—we told him he needed to come stay with us. Depressed, he quietly agreed, and we took him up to Port St. Lucie and gave him our guestroom.

"I can't do this anymore, Robby," he said. "I can't live this way."

He also told me, "Robby, you need to get those guns out of this house." He meant a couple assault rifles that he had given to Jackie. He'd also given her some Samurai swords from his antique collection. "They're not safe here," he said.

"Why? There's nothing illegal about them, is there?"

"No. You just need to get them out of here."

He kept pressing me about it, so the next day we took them to his place.

That night when we got home from work, he asked me again, "Robby, did you get those guns out of the house?"

"Yeah, they're out of here. We took them to your place."

"Ok," he said, just lying there in bed.

The following day at work, installing shutters with Jackie, I got an eerie feeling, like something was wrong. "Have you talked to your dad?" I asked Jackie.

"No, let me try to call him."

She tried, but no answer.

I still had that eerie feeling, but hoped I was just imagining things. But I was worried, because I knew those kinds of feelings often came true for me. I could sometimes be around bad people and somehow just know right away that they were bad (even if they seemed good), or I could be around other people who seemed bad but know right away that they were okay. I get these crazy strong vibes and energies that just flow through my whole body and I *know*. I think this is a gift God gave me, which in the Bible is called the gift of discernment. It really came in handy—and got even stronger—when I went to prison, where there were so many people and situations to watch out for; there, I'm sure it saved my life.

We finished out our workday and drove home. When we pulled up to the house, it seemed like I could physically feel death present. I was still hoping it was all in my head, but I stayed back at my truck, pretending I was working on it, and let Jackie go in first.

She came running out of the house, all upset and saying, "My dad's not answering! Robby, you have to go check on him."

I went inside to the guest room and knocked. "Michael? Michael?"

No answer.

I opened the door, "Michael, you in here? Are you all right?"

I stepped in. All the guest room had in it was the futon Michael slept on and the computer. He was on the futon, all covered up with the black blankets.

"Michael?"

I took his arm from under the blankets to shake it and wake him—and it was cold as ice and hard as a rock! My heart leapt into my throat. I saw a .40 caliber Glock lying on his chest, and you won't believe what I did next: I picked it up just like I would if I was planning to shoot it! Finger on the trigger and everything! Why would I do that? First, I was in a state of shock; after grabbing that lifeless arm, my heart was pounding and my head spinning. Second, I had a replica .40 caliber Glock BB gun in the house, and my first thought was that Michael must have taken it to bed with him because he was so paranoid—until I drew back the slide and saw a hollow point bullet in the chamber!

I dropped the gun on the floor.

Then I saw the blood on the blankets, pulled them back, and saw that he had shot himself in the head. There was blood all over his mouth, blood all over everywhere—I won't describe it all....

... That night was a nightmare. Jackie bawling and beating on the ground. Cops swarming all over the house with yellow tape. I having to explain to detectives why they were going to find my fingerprints all over the gun.

The days that followed were scary for me, because I was constantly worried about my prints being on that gun. I knew I hadn't done anything wrong, but I was stressed out. I didn't exactly have a great relationship with the cops at that time.

Then one day the detective called me and told me to come in! I was sweating bullets as they put me in an interrogation room, just like the ones you see in *The First 48,* and slid a manilla envelope across the table and said, "Take a look at those."

It was a bunch of pictures of Michael lying dead on the futon.

"Where was the gun when you found it?"

So I explained it to them. I don't think they ever really suspected me—rigor mortis and other clues made it clear Michael had shot himself, probably by pulling the trigger with his thumb, after pulling the blankets over his head—but they watched me closely as I talked.

Jackie's brother got out of prison on a furlough to come to the funeral. Jackie stayed depressed for months and months. We never stayed in that house again, but moved to another one not far away.

It was all very sad.

CHAPTER 9: At Gunpoint

For the love of money is a root of all kinds of evil –
1 Timothy 6:10

About this time, I started to hang out with Bryce and Russ again, as I tended to do whenever I got off the hardcore drugs. Russ's steroids "business" was really taking off (Bryce was back and forth between Florida and the West Coast in those days; he'd gone out there to work for his dad's company). Russ had come a long way from selling steroids out of his bedroom to fellow high schoolers; he had opened the Sun State Revitalization Clinic and was selling a literal fortune's worth of juice to customers all over the nation.

Here's how his scheme worked. He placed ads on the Internet aimed at men "Feeling tired? Low sex drive? Putting on fat?"—that sort of thing. When men clicked on the ads, they became a lead and Russ's telemarketers, fifteen to twenty musclebound guys at the "clinic" (an office building by a strip club), contacted them. They told the leads that all they had to do was get their blood work done and send the results to the clinic. Then the clinic's doctors would review the blood work results— Russ had roped a couple dishonest MDs into the scheme—diagnose them as low testosterone, and sign a prescription for steroids for them. The prescriptions were sent to a California pharmacy, who FedExed the drug to the customers. The clinic pocketed between $1,000 to $4,000 per customer, depending on the amounts of steroids purchased.

When I saw that kind of money rolling in, I wanted in

79

on it, and so I became one of Russ's telemarketers. Right away, I killed it—it's not hard to sell steroids to guys who want them! I kept my shutters and AC businesses going, hiring others to run them, but spent my time at the clinic. I quickly became one of Russ's top salesmen.

About this time, I left Jackie. We were fighting all the time, and I was tired of the drive, so one day I just up and left her. I left her the dogs, the furniture, everything—I didn't care. I found an apartment in Wellington, my old stomping grounds and nearer Russ's clinic.

I was making money fast now—from my shutters business, my AC company, and especially my steroids sales—and it became my newest addiction. Money, that is. When I saw some of the high-end vehicles Russ was buying, I decided to follow suit. I purchased a brand-new Cadillac Escalade pickup with a chameleon paint job. Other guys from our school days had sniffed out the money too, and we were all selling steroids at the clinic and making good money.

It Was On!

One day I walked out of the clinic to get something from my truck and saw a black Escalade SUV with sweet rims in the lot, a bald-headed dude sitting behind the wheel, his tattooed arm—sporting a diamond-studded Rolex Presidential—hanging out the window. He turned to look at me, pulled his Gucci sunglasses down, and said, "Robby!"

I looked closely and it was Luke Nelson, my old buddy from the Fern House.

"Luke!" I said, walking over.

"What's up, bro?" he said.

We caught up for a few moments, then I nodded at his watch and the Escalade. "How are you making all this money?"

"I told you what I was going to do. Don't you remember?"

Luke and I were always chopping it up at the Fern House, talking over crazy ideas. One of them was to make money off all the people trying to get out of their expensive timeshares that they never used.

"That's what I'm doing," Luke said. "I'm making all kinds of money. I've got multiple offices. Remember how we used to talk about how we were going to do it together? Man, I haven't seen you in a long time. Listen, bro, I'm going to help you start one."

He said it would take about $10,000 to open an office, but he would supply the leads and the telemarketers to get me started.

"$10,000?" I said. "I can make that happen."

I started hustling. I found an office building just down the street from the Fern House and paid the first and last months' rent (it was a dump; I called it the Roach Hotel). I bought a bunch of fold-out tables, roll-around office chairs, and cubicle partitions. I found a twenty-line phone system on Craigslist and called Florida Power & Light to come turn on the lights.

I told Luke I was ready and he was true to his word. He sent me about fifteen telemarketers, a list of leads to call, and a script to read to them. I had spent my $10,000 setting everything up, but the first week I made $25,000. It was on!

The script the telemarketers used went something like

this: "Hi, this is Robby with Worldwide Marketing Solutions. Do you have a timeshare in Orlando? When's the last time you used it? Wow, that's a long time. What kind of maintenance fees are you paying on that each month? Ouch! What if I told you I had a buyer who would pay you $20,000 for it today? Would you be interested? Well, I've got good news for you...." The telemarketer would tell them that we had the buyer and we had that price, and all we needed from them was some prepaid closing costs, $1,500 to $2,500, for a deed and title search and so forth. "You'll get that money back after the sale of the property, and then we will get our commission off that. We take Visa, MasterCard, and American Express."

People went for it—in droves. Within a month I was pocketing $50,000 a week. That kind of money goes to your head. One day I walked into a car dealership and bought a white Mercedes SL 500 *and* a red Ferrari 360 Modena. It was crazy.

I did all this—setting up the office and timeshare scam—without telling Bryce and Russ a thing. I knew they were touchy about anyone else making money like they did. I brought in a partner—a computer whiz named Jim Mitchell—to run the office when I wasn't there and meantime I continued to work at Russ's office in the day and hang out with him at night.

"We're Going to Kill You."

One day Russ said to me, "Man, I'm going to start a pain clinic. There's got to be a bunch of money in that. Everybody is buying all these pain pills from doctors. I could capitalize on that. I saw how bad you got on them, so I know other people are doing the same thing, spending all their money."

The next thing I knew he had opened his first pain clinic, in Fort Lauderdale. Eventually he and Bryce would open five clinics throughout South Florida, the largest of which was called U.S. Relief. They would become known as the kingpins of "Pain Lane," operators of the biggest "pill mill" in the country, according to later prosecutors. The way it worked is they found a building, called it a "pain clinic," hired doctors willing to write pain med prescriptions all day long, and threw open the doors to "patients." It brought in so much cash—$50,000 to $60,000 *a day*—that Bryce and Russ literally did not know what to do with it, stuffing it in duffel bags all over the place, hiding it in their mom's attic (ultimately, investigators would find $4.5 million there), and piling it up out in the open on pieces of furniture.

The more money Russ made, the crazier he got about it. I mean, paranoid—he and Bryce were always suspecting that people were stealing from them. So one night, when Russ received a call from Bryce saying that someone had stolen $500,000, Russ headed straight over. I was with him, and when we pulled up to their mom's house—in his midnight-black Cadillac XLR convertible—everyone was there: Bryce and all the "hangers-on," that is, the guys from high school who had started hanging around the clinics.

"I called the police," Bryce said.

"Why would you call the cops?" Russ said. "Are you crazy? We don't call cops; we're above the law."

"I want DNA and fingerprints," Bryce said.

Russ turned to me: "Robby, get the bag and gun out of here."

There was a duffel bag full of cash and a chrome 45 with a wood grain handle in the car. I snatched them and ran out to the woods behind their house with them. By the time I got back the cops were there and checking out the house. The twins' mom, who was divorced from their dad, had a normal little three-bedroom house in Wellington, maybe 1,800 square feet. Bryce and Russ stashed cash there because they thought no one would suspect it.

The police looked around and took a DNA swab from each of us, but basically said there was nothing they could do. Frankly, I don't think they cared too much about helping Bryce and Russ, because they knew about their law-breaking ways. They wrote their report and left.

Like I said, Bryce and Russ never trusted anyone, even their friends. So the next day I came up with the idea of giving everyone a lie detector test. Russ liked the idea, so he did some research and found a private investigator—a retired police detective—who gave the tests, and who used all the same equipment that cops and FBI agents used.

The day of the test—a couple hours before the retired cop showed up—Russ said to me, "Hey, bro, can you help me? Can you drive my Maserati from my mom's house to my house?"

"Yes!" I said, so he drove me over, gave me the keys, and I climbed in and started driving back to his house, where the lie detector test was going to be given. I was enjoying the drive—it was a pearl-white, souped-up Maserati—and for some reason I happened to open the center console and there inside it was a stack of crisp $100 bills. I thumbed through it and estimated that it contained about $25,000.

Now I'd never stolen anything from Bryce or Russ, but there in the Maserati I peeled off about $10,000 in bills and put them in my pocket. The reason I did it (or at least the excuse I gave myself) was because Russ was continually beating up my paycheck at the revitalization clinic. If I had $5,000 coming to me from selling steroids, he'd make up some reason to take $1,000 off the top. So I took the money.

When I got to Russ's house, the examiner was there with his equipment. Four of us would be taking the test, but not Bryce and Russ. The test was given in the first-floor office. I was called in last. It was just me and the examiner, a gray-haired dude who looked more like a retired science teacher than a detective. He strapped me in: a tube around my chest to measure my respiratory rate, a blood pressure cuff around my upper arm to measure blood pressure and heart rate, and two fingerplates to measure perspiration on my fingertips.

I took a deep breath. "Man, I'm really nervous," I said to the examiner. "Will that make me fail?"

"No, not at all. Now look straight ahead and answer yes or no to the following questions. Is your last name Eddy?"

"Yes."

"Do you intend to lie to any of the questions on this test?"

"No."

"Is the sky blue?"

"Yes."

"Is the grass green?"

"Yes."

"Did you steal the $500,000 in question?"

"No."

"Have you ever stolen *any* money from Bryce or Russ Owen?"

"No."

And so on, about fifteen questions.

When it was all over, the examiner met privately with Bryce and Russ for a few moments, then we all went out to lunch. Bryce and Russ didn't say anything, so I assumed we had all passed. "Hey, why don't we go out on the airboat today?" Russ said.

"Yeah, let's do it!"

We headed back to Russ's house to get ready. "I don't have any board shorts," I said when we walked in.

"Go upstairs and grab some from my closet," Russ said.

I went upstairs and into his room. One thing that was strange about Russ is that, though he lived in this multi-million dollar home, he didn't care much about furniture. His bed was just a mattress on the floor with a blanket on it. There was a huge pile of money on the floor near the closet; it must have been a four-feet by four-feet stack; there was probably a half-$1 million right there.

I entered the closet to get the board shorts, and as I turned back around, there they were: Bryce, Russ, and the hangers-on—and Bryce and Russ were pointing guns at me! Russ held a snub nose .357 Magnum with no hammer, Bryce a .40 caliber Glock. Bryce also pointed a big can of pepper spray at me.

"Don't move or we'll shoot you!"

"Put the cuffs on him."

One of the hangers-on slapped cuffs on me behind my back.

"Get on your knees!"

I did it, but of course the whole time I'm shocked and terrified, protesting, "What is this? What's going on?"

"You failed the lie detector test, Robby! Where's the money?"

"I didn't take the money!"

Russ walked over and pushed me down on my stomach on the tan carpet.

"You failed the lie detector test! You better tell us right now, we're going to kill you."

I found out later that I passed on all the questions except one: if I had *ever* stolen from Bryce and Russ. Because I had stolen that $10,000 from Russ's Lamborghini on my way to take the test! And *I* had been the one to suggest the lie detector test. These were ironies I had no time to appreciate at that moment.

Russ put the gun to my head and spread his other hand out over my head like a shield, as though to keep my blood from splattering all over the place when he shot me.

"Shoot him, Russ!" Bryce was saying. "Shoot! We'll take his body to the Everglades and the gators will eat him up."

I thought I was going to die. I was crying and I literally soiled my pants. "I don't have your money! I don't have your money!" I thought of making up some lie about where the money was to buy some time and get a chance to escape.

Boom! Boom! Boom! Russ fired the gun three times right by my head. (He would later regret this, as the FBI, in their eventual investigations of the twins, would find the bullets lodged in the concrete under the carpet).

They pulled me to my feet, got Jackie on my speaker phone, and told me to ask her where the money was.

"Jackie," I said, "where's the money?"

"I have no idea what you're talking about," she said. "What are you talking about?"

"Jackie, where's the money?"

"Robby, what's wrong with you? I don't know what you're talking about."

Russ grabbed the phone and threw it.

They realized then that I had not taken the money, and started to say, "We were just messing with you, Robby. It was a scare tactic. We just wanted to make sure you didn't do it."

My fear was turning to fury. As soon as they took the cuffs off me, I headed straight downstairs and outside to my truck, where I had a .40 caliber Glock in the center console. I grabbed it, went back inside and upstairs, cocked it, and started firing at them.

Click. Click. Click.

There were no bullets in the gun. Beforehand, they had gotten into my truck and removed the clip; I had been too upset to notice. (Thank God they had done it! I would have had those killings on my conscience, and who knows what legal consequences I would have faced. It was one more miracle of provision and protection in my life.)

I dropped the gun on the floor. I went down the stairs, got in my truck, and drove off.

CHAPTER 10: Downhill Fast

As a dog returns to its vomit, so fools repeat their folly – Proverbs 26:11

I was done with Bryce and Russ, of course—though, as you'll see, they were still thinking *a lot* about me. I was making plenty of money on my own and didn't need them. When our paths crossed occasionally at a strip club, it was tense. Not only because we hated each other, but because of paranoia: Neither party was sure what the other might do.

High Roller

Greed and pride fueled my lifestyle in those days. After swindling people by day, at night I would drive up to the strip clubs in my red Ferrari, pull up right in front with hundreds of dollars in my hand for the valet, and make sure all eyes were on me as I stepped out of my vehicle in my Ferragamo shoes, Gucci belt, True Religion jeans, and Rolex Yacht-Master watch with a diamond dial on my wrist. I walked through the doors like I owned the place, skipping all lines as I tossed bills at bouncers and managers and went straight to the roped-off VIP tables. All the girls would fight to get over to me, because I was young and good-looking and—most important—swimming in cash. It all fueled my ego; I felt like I was on top of the world.

All the managers knew me because I burned so much money in their places. One night I called one over. "Hey, how about we shut this place down except for me and my buddies here?" I said.

"I can't do that, bro," he said.

I went out to my Ferrari, grabbed an envelope with $25,000 cash in it, and brought it back in. I handed it to him. "Now can you?" I said.

Needless to say, he shut it down.

I got a call one day telling me that Luke Nelson—my friend from the Fern House—had died. He had OD'd while speedballing in some hotel on Belvedere Road. I was shocked and saddened. Luke had his problems, but he had always been open-hearted to me.

A week or so later his ex-wife, Allison, came bursting into the office with a couple musclebound dudes. She got everyone's attention and said, "Now that Luke is dead, I'm shutting this office down. We don't need it. Everybody needs to come with me."

I had been expecting something like this. Allison and I had never gotten along, and it chafed her that Luke helped me get started.

"Hold it," I said to everybody. "I'm not shutting anything down. I'm opening an account at the bank under my own company's name, which I've already picked out. Stay, and I'll double your pay, from five percent commission to ten percent."

That put an end (temporarily) to Allison's plans against me, and before long my new company was crushing it, making twice as much as before. We moved to a big warehouse and built a bunch of offices in it for the telemarketers, over sixty of them eventually, each bringing in $1,500 to $2,500 per close. Jim and I had our own massive office, each with our own L-shaped presidential desk. We watched a sixty-inch flatscreen TV that monitored every single thing a telemarketer said or did, for we had a camera and a microphone aimed at each desk.

I moved into an enormous two-story, seven-bedroom house in the Olympia development of Wellington, an upscale neighborhood. I moved in all alone. The house came completely furnished, and I threw big parties and told everybody I owned it all, though I was actually paying $5,000 a month in rent. I parked five vehicles in the driveway and a bunch of Harleys and four-wheelers in the garage, paying about $7,000 a month in leases for the vehicles.

All this time I hadn't taken a drink or done any hardcore drugs, not since going to jail for my fight with Jackie. But the fateful night came, and it came at a strip club—let me say something about strip clubs here:

You've probably noticed that whenever I wasn't living right, that's where I spent my time—at strip clubs. It wasn't just because of the girls, but because those places really are the devil's den, where every dark deed—substance abuse, drug deals, prostitution, all kinds of crimes—are not only permitted but condoned. Don't let the flashing lights and seductive signs fool you. People go to those places to hurt and be hurt. That's why I went to them constantly when I wasn't living right: I felt right at home in them.

It was at one that a tall, dark-haired girl said to me one night, "Why can't you just have a drink with me? Just have one drink." And though I *knew* the pain and destruction that always followed alcohol into my life, though I had lived it first-hand repeatedly, somehow here came that mental blank spot, that selective amnesia—and I forgot it all. The cunning and powerful foe of alcoholism had struck again, and I took the drink.

Of course, I ended up black-out drunk that night. Of course, I kept drinking on the following nights. Eventually, I was going to the clubs every night, not just on the weekends.

Every once in a while, I got the idea to go to some other country and would hop on a plane with my "friends"—i.e., employees—and go to Costa Rica or Brazil or somewhere like that. We would strut around those Third World countries in our *Norte Americano* clothes and expensive shoes and watches and with our pockets full of cash. When a waitress asked if we wanted something to drink, we answered, "We don't want *some*thing to drink—we want bottles and bottles!" In Bogota, Colombia, I started using hardcore drugs again, buying some high-powered cocaine on the street for $50. We were almost killed in Colombia. We'd gone to a party at some drug lord's mansion—six stories, a spiral staircase of marble, machine gun-toting guards in black fatigues out front—and made no friends (fooling around with their women and showing off our money). The next night, in a cab on the way to a club, the driver told us nervously that we should not go there. "The cartel is looking to kill the rich white boys." We turned the cab around and got out of the country as fast as we could.

Going Downhill

Back in the States, my problems were just beginning.

At the office, our whole database was stolen and taken to Allison, all of our leads and "clients." This was a serious problem because Allison would call everyone who had paid us money, tell them it was a scam, and then offer—for a fee—to recover that money for them. If she reached them before ninety days had passed, they could get a refund from our account, which we couldn't stop. The irony is that Allison was just scamming them again—she wasn't doing anything for that fee—but that didn't stop the money from draining out of our account. And the poor people we had swindled called us all day long, threatening to sue us, kill us, call the FBI. Some flew into Florida to try to knock on our doors, but I had purposely chosen a gated warehouse, and I even had security patrolling outside.

One day we were in fact raided. I had just unlocked the door and stepped outside—to go to the store and buy some alcohol—when a guy with a badge came up to me.

"Who are you?" he demanded.

"I'm the maintenance man," I said.

"Are there other people in there?"

"Yeah, a bunch of people working. I'm just the maintenance man."

"Get out of here quick, because we're going in."

I got out of there quick.

Later Jim told me that agents and cops came scrambling in, combing through documents, asking about a business license, collecting any evidence they could of a scam. Believe it or not, after they left, we kept right on making calls! We were in too deep to stop now. Besides, in the very fine print of the paperwork we sent to "clients" was the declaration that we weren't promising to sell their timeshare but just to market it (of course, we weren't doing that either). It was a thin straw to hang our hopes on, but it was all we had.

The upshot was that our income, once pouring into the account like a firehose, had become a *drip, drip, drip.*

We lost employees. My lavish lifestyle became impossible to maintain. The repo man came knocking for the vehicles and the real owner of the house for his rent money. Ultimately, I had to move into an efficiency apartment. As the money went, so did my "friends"— gone! Even the strippers wanted nothing to do with me. I became a Lone Wolf, drinking by myself until I blacked out or climbed into my vehicle to drive home. I got another DUI; lost my license; but kept driving. I started coming into the office later and later, and Jim was losing patience with me.

As my problems mounted, I only increased my drinking and drug use—it was the only way I could feel better. I would go off the Suboxone for a few days so I could take opiates and get some peace. I even ground down Roxicodone tablets—an extended-release form of oxycodone—so I could shoot it in my veins. I stayed drunk or high all day long. When I did get a little money, I went straight to the strip club and spent it on drinks or drugs. One time I bought five Ecstasy pills from a drug dealer, popped them immediately in my mouth, and chewed them down. The *drug dealer* looked at me with concern and said, "Man, you need to slow down!"

But I got worse and worse, so bad that when I learned my dad was going to need a liver transplant, I could barely take an interest. Jackie moved back in with me— in the efficiency apartment—and we drank together and fought. In the morning I would down three Xanax tablets to come down from the cocaine (one of those pills will lay a normal person out). Then I would go to the Chevron across the street and fill a 32-ounce cup with ice. I would buy two big cans of Four Loco—a stiff alcoholic beverage, which at the time was also marketed as an energy drink—and pour them in the cup. I would arrive at the office already hammered.

Murder-for-Hire

By now we were down to just a few employees, and I was desperately trying to find new leads. At the same time, I heard that Bryce and Russ were getting bigger and bigger, making more and more money with their pain clinics. I even heard that they had opened up a "timeshare" call center with Allison as a partner. I wondered if they did it just to spite me, since they didn't need the money.

One day I was driving on Palm Beach Lakes Blvd when two Dodge Chargers pulled up beside me—one silver and one black. One of the guys—an FBI agent—rolled down his window and told me to pull over. I turned into a Home Depot. I thought I was in big trouble, but all they asked me about was Bryce and Russ. Had they tried to contact me? Had I heard anything about them to trying to kill me?

I told them I didn't know anything about that.

They put me in the back of one of their cars, then one of them walked around my Range Rover; he had a pole with a mirror on the end and he was checking under the vehicle.

"What are you doing? I asked.

"Looking for bombs or tracking devices."

They asked me a bunch of questions, but I didn't know anything to tell them. Even if I had, I wouldn't have told them anything. The criminal's code against snitching ran deep in me, even snitching against Bryce and Russ.

The agents told me to watch the news tomorrow and

let me go. The next morning Bryce and Russ were all over the TV news. Their pain clinics, houses—everything—had been raided by the FBI, and Bryce and Russ arrested. All right there on the TV. It barely phased me as I went through my morning routine of eating Xanax and drinking Four Locos.

When I got to the office, Jim was holding a copy of the *Palm Beach Post.* "Dude, you better get your life together," he said to me, which was funny coming from a guy scamming people for a living.

He tossed the paper on the desk in front of me. There, in the front page story about Bryce and Russ, was my name. It said the judge had let Russ Owen out on a bond, but not Bryce Owen. Bryce had been caught on wire trying to arrange the murder-for-hire of "John Robert Eddy"!

CHAPTER 11: "Have You Had Enough?"

In my distress I called to the Lord, and he answered me – Jonah 2:2

B elieve it or not, I was so bad on drugs and alcohol, that what I read in the paper didn't even phase me.

I suppose Bryce never got over the fear that I might report them to the police for what they did to me. (The official indictment for their crime against me would say that they "unlawfully kidnapped, abducted and imprisoned" me "and committed an aggravated assault with a firearm.") So Bryce decided to pay one of our mutual childhood friends a few hundred thousand (I never learned the exact amount) to kill me, but that friend was wearing a wire for the FBI. He had been involved in Bryce and Russ's illegal operations, and so the FBI approached him and said he was going away for a long time if he didn't cooperate with them. So he was wearing the wire that recorded Bryce's offer to pay for my murder. The crazy thing is, I never had any intention of going to the police.

But before I'd finished reading the article Jim had put in front of me, I was already thinking about my next drink or drug. I had become a full-blown alcoholic. I spent a few hours at the office, drinking Four Loco from my giant soft drink cup, then headed to the liquor store for a handle of Ketel One Vodka or Captain Morgan. I spent the rest of the day drinking. As for drugs, I took everything I could get my hands on: cocaine, Xanax,

Ecstasy, opiates—it didn't matter. I was a "garbage can," my drug of choice "more."

Out-of-Body

One night I bought some GHB from a guy at a strip club. I hadn't used this drug in a long time, not since OD'ing on it (in the superglue remover) several years back. The next morning in our apartment, after I was already high and drunk, I grabbed the bottle of GHB, unscrewed the lid, and poured myself a capful, then another—and suddenly realized I had taken too much.

I was overdosing, slipping away—and there was nothing I could do about it.

I remember thinking, *You really messed up now. You took too much. You're dying!*

It was incredibly scary. I knew what was happening but was totally helpless.

People say your life flashes before your eyes before you die. I really did think of my mom and dad and how I had ruined my life.

The next thing I knew I was in the back of an ambulance, paramedics working feverishly over me, saying, "Hey, stay with us! Stay with us!" Then I found myself *looking down* on them as they cut away my clothes; as they sprayed NARCAN up my nose; as they applied the defibrillator paddles to my chest; and as they jolted me with the electricity. I saw Jackie there (she had called them), crying her eyes out. I would be sober two years before I realized I had been *looking down* on all this, from outside my body. I was that close to dying.

I returned to consciousness in the hospital room hooked up to a bunch of machines. I had a tube in my nose, another down my throat, an IV in my arm, a catheter. But all I could think was, *Get me out of this place. I've got to go get drunk or high.* And as soon as I got out, that's exactly what I went to do.

All my walls were down, my defenses gone. I was helpless against my powerful and cunning foe of alcoholism. And it was zeroing in for the kill.

I had warrants out for my arrest in three counties. (I was twenty-eight years old and had been arrested in a total of seven Florida counties so far: Hendry, Lee, Okaloosa, Orange, Palm Beach, Martin, and St. Lucie.) I had a variety of crimes on my record, including DUIs, trespassing, drug charges, driving on a revoked license, reckless driving, theft, battery, a weapons charge. I wouldn't go to any court dates, so I had a bunch of "failures to appear" hanging over my head as well. All of these worries only made me drink and drug more. I became paranoid about driving my own car, for fear of being pulled over, so I would ask people to switch cars with me. Because they got to drive my high-end vehicle while I took their piece of junk, they said, "Sure!" I even used a friend's ID to buy a new car, a Mercedes E 350. It worked because we looked alike. The next day I rammed it into the rear-end of another vehicle on the I-95 exit ramp. I got out and saw that the driver was okay and said to her, "Please, don't call the cops. I'll just pay for it."

She got on the line to her husband, then told me, "My husband says I have to call the police."

"Ok. No problem."

I walked behind the Mercedes, folded up the temporary tag so it couldn't be read, then jumped in the car and drove off. It was just one of several hit-and-runs I committed, thankfully (miraculously!) all minor fender-benders. Usually I literally ran away on foot before the cops got there, leaving the car I'd borrowed at the scene.

"Have You Had Enough?"

By now I didn't even look like myself. Sometimes I show people photos taken of me in those days and they can't believe the person in the photo was really me. I was an empty shell, living for and on nothing but alcohol and drugs.

I can hardly remember how it happened, but I ended up one day at a pawnshop on Dixie Highway trying to hawk an expensive Breitling watch. I had bought it in my high-rolling days for something like $5,000, but here I was ready to part with it for pennies on the dollar. But the pawnshop workers took one look at me and figured I must have stolen it. They gave me a hard time, asking a bunch of suspicious questions. I ended up just walking out with the watch and getting in my car.

As soon as I pulled onto Dixie Highway, I saw the familiar blue and red lights flashing in my mirror, this time from an unmarked Crown Vic. I had given the pawnshop people my name and an ID, and they must have called the cops.

I pulled over, and the Crown Vic stopped behind me. A plainclothes officer in a bulletproof vest stepped out—I knew he was from the warrant squad.

I knew I was going away. There I was, sitting behind the wheel of a vehicle totally drunk and high. I had all kinds of drugs in the car, pill bottles without any labels. I had no driver's license, no registration, no insurance. And then there were all the warrants, the reason this guy had been sent for me. I knew I was going away, and I knew the detox was going to be brutal, but a part of me was actually relieved; I was sick and tired of being sick and tired.

"Step out of the vehicle."

I cooperated with him. He ran my name and searched the car, finding all the drugs.

He was in his forties, with a military bearing and a muscular build. It was weird, though; he wasn't gruff with me, like most cops, but mild and very kind.

"Son!" he suddenly said, "Have you had enough? You're going to die! Listen. I'm only going to take you in for the warrants. Not the drugs or a DUI or anything else. Just the warrants."

I couldn't believe my ears. Even drunk and stoned, I knew I was being blessed.

"This is your last chance, buddy," he said. "God is saving you. Do the right thing."

Within the hour I was in a holding cell at the county jail. I talked to a nurse and told her how much I had been drinking and drugging and how bad I knew my detox was going to be, but she couldn't have cared less—I was just a criminal to her, so it was sink or swim. All they did was put me in the medical dorm, which, instead of two-man cells, has beds spread out in one large room like an ER unit. There were guys in there with everything from police dog bites to gunshot wounds.

Day two, the detox pains hit with a fury: uncontrollable shaking, nausea and puking, blurred vision and confusion, anxiety and the sweats, aching all over, soiling my pants. In addition to coming down from drugs, I was experiencing the worst kind of alcohol withdrawal, the delirium tremens (DTs). Your brain, so used to the depressant effect of alcohol, goes haywire, blood pressure and heart rate spiking. People die from withdrawals; I almost did.

Day three, I had seizures. I was lying on my bed when a wave of weakness washed over me, my vision danced, and I blacked out.

Completely.

My next moment of consciousness I was sitting on the dorm floor, breathing like a madman, blood all over my blue scrubs, my teeth and jaw aching, my tongue almost bit in two, and my hands cuffed. Standing over me was a big black dude in black fatigues—he must have been six-foot-eight, 300 pounds. He was a member of the "goon squad," the special guards called in when something bad was going on in the dorms. He looked down at me warily, his massive arms crossed, blue medical gloves on his hands.

"You had a seizure," he said. "You almost bit your tongue off."

I learned later that I'd gone crazy, throwing detention officers and inmates all over the place.

As I sat there, another seizure hit....

This time I returned to consciousness in a big white cell with a padded floor. There were no bars, and it had no furniture—bunks, chairs, or anything. I was wearing a paper gown and was naked underneath. They started giving me Valium to taper off the barbiturate withdrawals. I had trouble sleeping, and I was hallucinating (I kept seeing a cop come to the door, open it, and tell me I could go home, but he had a rifle behind his back).

After a week they brought me out. Then, a week or so later, just when I was starting to feel a little better, they put me in shackles with a bunch of other guys, loaded us onto a Sheriff's Office bus, and transported us to another facility, the Stockade, an ancient jail near the South Florida Fairgrounds. (The Stockade gained some notoriety for housing the late financier and sex offender Jeffrey Epstein in his first incarceration.)

For some reason, they housed me in a dorm with "weekenders," inmates who lived outside during the week and reported to jail on Friday night. Some of them smuggled drugs back inside with them, and believe it or not—though I was just starting to get over a detox that almost killed me—I immediately hooked up with them. I was getting high on Xanax, pain pills, pot—even the psych meds of some of the inmates, which I bartered for. I was getting drunk too, because inmates know how to turn leftover fruit, sugar smuggled from the kitchen, and yeast from bread or biscuits into "hooch." I was getting as totally messed up in jail as I had been on the streets.

On the night of March 25, 2011—my twenty-ninth birthday—I once again hit my bunk as drunk and high as possible. But as I lay in the dark, I felt only sadness and depression. I kept remembering what my dad had said to me that day:

"Son, I can't stop you from killing yourself. But I'm not going to let you kill your mother. We're done. Don't write. Don't call. We're done, Son."

I thought about all the misery I had caused my parents through the years, and how they should have written me off a long time ago. The weight of the world seemed to lay on my chest.

Then a Voice spoke to me: "You've lost everything in your life. Your family. Your money. You can't even make phone calls." (I didn't have money on my jail account to place calls or buy anything from the canteen.) "Look at all this you have lost," the Voice said, "and now you can't even stay sober in a controlled environment." But it wasn't a mean voice; it was peaceful somehow—and it broke my heart.

I started to cry.

I got down on my knees beside the bunk and said, "Please, God. Whoever's out there." (I didn't even know if I believed in God. I just knew I was helpless, totally defeated.) "Please help me stay clean and sober. Please help me stop drinking and drugging. I can't do this anymore."

I meant every word.

And the crazy thing is, there on my knees, a miracle happened....

CHAPTER 12: Miracle

All things are possible with God – Mark 10:27

R ight there on my knees, my desire—my obsession—to drink and drug was literally snatched away from me! God took it away. Somehow I knew it was all over. I felt peace.
And I haven't had a drink or a drug since.
Like I said, a miracle happened.

Getting Sober in Rough Conditions

Of course, I didn't know then that I would stay clean and sober all these years since that moment. I just knew God had answered my prayer, and I was serious about it. I still had to get sober in some very rough conditions—a jail full of users and plenty of alcohol and drugs to go around. There were no Twelve-Step meetings to attend, but thankfully I knew enough from my Fern House days to do the most basic things:

I started each day on my knees in prayer, and hit my knees often during the day, asking God to help me stay sober. I did it right in front of the other prisoners; I didn't care who was watching. And then I prayed on my knees every night, thanking him for helping me stay sober that day. From somewhere I found a copy of the Big Book, the Twelve-Steppers guide to sobriety, and read it religiously.

I did all this day after day for the rest of my time at the Stockade. My health was still in the slow process of recovering from all the abuse I had put it through; it would take about eight months before I could sleep a full night and stopped shaking completely. I slowly started working out again in my cell, but I could barely do four or five pushups, and this after all my intense training through the years.

My sentence was completed in about eight months, but that didn't mean I was getting out of jail. I still had the Martin County warrants hanging over my head. So they put me in a police van and drove me up I-95 to Stuart, Florida, and the Martin County Jail. I immediately got a job there in the jail kitchen, which helped to break up the time. I would work in the kitchen all day, go back to my cell at night, work out, read the Big Book, pray, and go to sleep.

At Martin County, I was still getting sober in rough conditions, but at least there was one Twelve-Step meeting each month. But I was the only man in the jail who went to it. The detention officers would call out "Outside Meeting," and I was the only one who stood up and went into the classroom. The guy who brought the meeting into the jail was an older, gray-haired man. I often think about him because he was a part of saving my life. He could have been home with his family, but he was sacrificing an evening of his life to come help one guy he didn't even know. He read the Big Book with me and talked to me.

We did that for about a year. When I was about to get released, he said, "Robby, I need to tell you something. The first twenty-four hours after you leave this place are going to determine whether you stay sober or not. As soon as you leave here, go straight to a Twelve-Step meeting, get a sponsor, and start to work the steps immediately."

Every other time when I was about to get out of jail,

that was the last thing I was thinking about doing. Instead, I'd be thinking about meeting some girl or getting some non-jail food or sleeping in my own bed. But this time I listened to him like my life depended on it, because I finally realized *it did*. It's pretty crazy. All those drug overdoses, hospitalizations, lock-ups, near-death experiences—and I was only now realizing my life was on the line! That's the deceptive power of alcoholism and addiction, the diseases that deny their own existence.

First Steps

When I got out, and my mom and dad picked me up at the jail, I literally did exactly what that man told me to do. I had my parents take me straight to a Twelve-Step meeting at a little strip mall in West Palm Beach. And once inside the meeting I walked right up to the first man I saw and asked if he'd be my sponsor. "I just got out of jail," I said, "and I'm scared, and dying from alcoholism."

It may sound crazy or extreme that I did these things literally on the way home from jail, but I might not be sober today if I hadn't. How many men and women get out of jail each week, with all kinds of plans to stay sober, only to find themselves drunk or high before the day is out?

Though I asked the first guy I saw to be my sponsor, he turned me down for some reason or another and sent me to someone else, and I actually had trouble finding a sponsor those first few weeks out of jail. I went through two or three guys whose walk did not match their talk, who talked a good game in meetings but lived like something else outside. Those were hard and scary days for me. Trying to stay sober. Trying to find a sponsor. Trying to get to meetings without a driver's license. Trying to find a job without a driver's license. I was so used to living like a criminal, but now I had to find another way. I remember one day just lingering in the shower, letting the water rain down over me, worrying about how I was going to do it all.

More Miracles

But I was about to learn that God had my back. If he knows you're serious, that you're really *done* with the old ways, he'll do miracles to help you out. One for me was getting a job. I got dressed up in some good-looking clothes (to make a good first impression, like my dad taught me) and walked into Airstar Air Conditioning in Jupiter and handed them my resume. I told them that I was very good at air conditioning, that I could do it all—installs, repairs, ductwork, ice machines, etc.—and they were duly impressed. "But here's the bad news," I said, determined to be honest, "I just got out of jail and don't have a driver's license. But you can pay me less, give me a driver, and I *promise* I'll run circles around everyone you've got here."

Believe it or not, they hired me! Now I am an AC contractor and have worked for years in the business, and let me tell you: *No one* gets hired without a driver's license. It just won't happen. Ever.

But it did.

Another miracle happened to help me find my sponsor. I was staying for a couple days with the latest guy who had volunteered to be my sponsor, but I quickly found out he wasn't legit. He immediately was inviting female "newcomers"—women just starting to attend

Twelve Step meetings—over to his house to hit on them at this vulnerable time in their life. He was trying to have me do it too. I would never in a million years be part of something like that. I prayed that night, "God, please help me. I need a real sponsor. Please put one in my life."

The very next day, when I got to the job site—an old house that was being renovated—who did I see? None other than Larry Brunell! You remember when I took my first stab at sobriety—back in Chapter 6, when I really wasn't all-in, but kept hanging onto a "little" crookedness—I mentioned a group of hardcore sponsors who took the Twelve Steps as seriously as they used to take their drinking and drugging? Well, Larry was one of these guys!

I went straight up to him (it was his company doing the renovating) and asked him if he would be my sponsor. Now Larry, when you get to know him, has a heart as big as the sea, but at first glance he can be a little intimidating; he has a gruff, no-nonsense exterior. And he's as blunt as a board; he will always tell you the truth, even if it hurts. He looked closely at me with those clear blue eyes and finally said, "Yes, I will help you."

I breathed a sigh of relief. This was the answer to my prayer.

"But there are conditions," he said. "I'm going to take you through the Big Book paragraph by paragraph, and I'm not going to put a spin on it. What it says to do, we're going to do. It's the instruction manual, directions on how to get and stay sober."

"I'll do that. I need that."

"I want you to call me every day with your thoughts, your plans, and your ideas. And I want you to go to meetings every day. My sponsor goes to meetings every day, and I go to meetings every day, and we've been sober for years and years."

"I'll do it."

"By the way, Robby, you don't have to sign up for any of this. You can do anything you want. But if you want me to be your sponsor, these are the things you are going to have to do. Otherwise, we can just stay friends; it's no big deal, bud."

I was desperate, out of options, so of course I would sign up for all that. "I'm in," I said.

I needed a guy like that. I didn't need a guy who was going to pat me on the back and tell me everything was going to be okay. I needed a guy who was man enough to tell me the truth about my alcoholism and help me save my life. I needed a hands-on sponsor. I needed someone who would take my hand and put it in God's hand, and that's exactly what Larry did.

As we began to work through the twelve steps, the miracles continued, and step by step my life kept getting better. I traveled all over the country making amends to people I had hurt (Step 9). I started reaching out to help other men like me (Step 12), which was a big part of keeping me sober and close to God. My relationships, my work, my health, my mind and emotions—everything was improving, and I saw nothing but blue skies on the horizon....

Then one day I was standing on a ladder in a customer's garage taping ductwork, and my cell phone rang. I saw that it was Jack Frizzell, who had been my lawyer since I started getting in trouble when I was seventeen. I had actually gone in to see him when I was making amends to people, and he was really proud of how I'd turned my life around. He would call every once in a while just to see how I was doing. Which is why I thought he was calling now. I was in for a surprise.

"Robby," he said, "I've got some bad news for you."

"Really? What?" I couldn't imagine what it could be.

"I've got a federal indictment right here in front of me. You've been indicted by the FBI."

CHAPTER 13: Indictment

No discipline seems pleasant at the time, but painful. Later on, however, it produces a harvest of righteousness and peace for those who have been trained by it – Hebrews 12:11

The indictment, entitled the "United States of America vs. John Robert Eddy," said:

Between 2007 and 2010 John Robert Eddy and other defendants, doing business as Universal Marketing Solutions, conducted a telemarketing timeshare resale scheme falsely representing to have found buyers for consumers' timeshare interests, soliciting fees of up to several thousand dollars from each consumer in purported pre-paid closing costs and related expenses. In fact, Eddy and other defendants simply pocketed the fees, collecting approximately $30 million and victimizing approximately 22,219 consumers in all fifty states, the District of Columbia and Puerto Rico; all ten Canadian provinces and the Northwest Territory of Canada.

Signed, Stephen R. Wigginton, United States Attorney

As Jack read the charges to me over the phone, I got nauseous and lightheaded, right there on the ladder.

"You better come in and see me," he said.

As I hung up, I felt like the sky was crashing down on me. But believe it or not, my first thought was not of a drink or a drug, but to call Larry, who I was used to talking to every day.

"It will all work out, Robby," he said. "God will have your back. Unfortunately, there are consequences to our actions. We have to man up and do the next right thing." Then he said, "By the way, I happen to have some experience with the FBI." He told me that he was a twice-convicted felon and had spent time in federal prison.

Somehow it made me feel better to know that Larry had been down this road before me. He was not my sponsor by accident.

Even so, when I went in to see my lawyer, I was scared, and at first the old Robby came out:

"We need to suit up!" I said. "Take this to trial. They never caught me doing anything. They've got nothing on me."

"Let me explain something to you, son," Jack said patiently. "Do you know anything about the feds? They've got a ninety-nine percent conviction rate. When they get you, they've got you. You're definitely guilty, and they've definitely got you, and you're definitely going to prison. Let's just try to get the least time possible."

I knew he was right. Especially the part about being "definitely guilty."

I calmed down, and we decided that the first thing I had to do was turn myself in.

Which was easier said than done. Because this was a federal case—I was charged with victimizing consumers in all fifty states!—and the investigation had originated in the Southern District of Illinois, I had to go all the way to Chicago to appear. I had only $500 to my name and couldn't afford to fly, so I rented a four-cylinder Toyota and made the 1,300-mile drive in two days, sleeping in the car.

I was scared, not knowing if they were going to lock me up on the spot or let me bond out. My heart dropped when the judge set my bond at $100,000, meaning I would have to put down $10,000, which might as well have been $10 million for me at that time. Then my first legal miracle occurred. The judge said he'd settle for my signature with a promise to appear! I guess he thought if I drove all the way up there to turn myself in, I wasn't a flight risk.

That was huge for me. The presentencing investigation would take a year, and I was able to spend that year working on my sobriety. I talked to Larry every day, went to meetings every day, and started to sponsor men and take meetings into institutions. I went into the CARP detox center, where a lot of hardcore street addicts come in for help. Helping other men with the same problems—being a "fisher of men"—helps keep me sober and close to God.

I worked on Step Nine that year, making amends to people I had hurt. I made trips to Boston, Texas.... I even traveled out to California to apologize to my sister and her husband. Something powerful spiritually takes place when you get things right with people. These trips were another legal miracle, because I had to get the okay from my pretrial release officer. He could have easily turned them down as an unnecessary flight risk.

Court

I learned that the prosecutor was seeking twenty-five years for my sentence, which just took my breath away. Twenty years for the crime itself, five more because it involved elderly victims. The feds use a points system to calculate sentence lengths. It takes into account past infractions, and of course I had plenty of those. I asked people from all the meetings I attended to write letters to the judge for me, telling him how I had changed my life. And I asked them to pray for me.

The sentencing took place in St. Louis. Larry, like a true foxhole buddy, went with me. When I woke up in the hotel on the morning of the hearing, my stomach was in knots. I got into my dress shirt and tie. When we were about to leave for the court building, my cell phone rang—and believe it or not, it was a telemarketer telling me I'd won some big prize somewhere and all I needed to do to collect it was send in a certain amount of money. I couldn't help but laugh. I handed the phone to Larry, and he started acting like he was buying every word of the script. I could actually hear the telemarketer getting more and more excited, thinking he was reeling in a big one. Larry went on and on with him until I was laughing so much my stomach hurt. It was just what I needed to relieve a little tension. Finally, the telemarketer realized Larry was joking and started cussing him out. We were both laughing as we headed out to court.

The hearing was held in the Thomas F. Eagleton United States Courthouse, which is the largest single courthouse in the nation, twenty-nine stories tall. It is an imposing sight when you're walking up to it to be sentenced by the government that occupies it. I had a lot going on inside me—worries and fears and questions—but somehow I had a peace too. I had truly given the whole situation to God, whatever the outcome. I knew I was in his hands.

We met my lawyer in the downstairs lobby. He

wasn't Jack, my personal lawyer from Florida. I couldn't afford a penny in legal expenses, so the feds had provided me with a local attorney. He, Larry, and I took the elevator up to the courtroom.

Larry was the only spectator, so he sat alone in the gallery. I sat with my lawyer at the defendant's table, the prosecutor sat at his table, the stenographer at her table, and the marshal stood.

"All rise," the marshal said when the judge entered.

The judge, a Reagan appointee, looked like he was about ninety years old. He was short and balding. He took his seat on the high judge's bench, and the hearing began.

The prosecutor spoke first, talking about all the bad things I had done and why I deserved twenty-five years. Then my lawyer spoke, pressing for ten years. And for a while my lawyer and the prosecutor went back and forth, volleying fifteen years of my life between them like a tennis ball, with the judge asking questions.

Finally, the prosecutor said, "Your Honor, as a part of our presentencing investigation, we interviewed a number of people who know or have known Mr. Eddy and were told without exception that he has become sober and turned over a new leaf on life. We are willing to drop our sentence request from twenty-five to ten years. In light of his extensive criminal history, that is as lenient as we can be. We acknowledge that he has changed, and we are happy about that, but the law is the law."

Out of nowhere, the judge looked at Larry in the gallery. "Mr. Brunell?" he said.

Surprised, Larry stood. "Yes, sir?"

"Will you take the stand, please?"

I looked at my lawyer, and he was just as surprised as Larry. He had mentioned, when talking about how my life had changed, that my sponsor had traveled to court with me from Florida, but no one was expecting the judge to call Larry to the stand.

The judge chatted with Larry a few moments—asking about his background, thanking him for coming, etc.—then said, "Do you think Mr. Eddy will stay sober?"

"Your Honor," Larry said, "I don't have a crystal ball. I can only tell you what Robby has been doing these last two years, which is work hard on his sobriety. Following the Twelve Steps. Going to meetings. Helping other men. If he keeps doing the things he has been doing, he will stay sober. If he doesn't, he will not stay sober."

The judge seemed surprised. He was probably used to hearing a bunch of bull from witnesses, telling him whatever they thought he wanted to hear. Larry was straight up with him.

He thanked Larry, who returned to the gallery.

Then the judge looked at me—it was my turn to speak.

I stood up, said a silent prayer asking God to speak through me, and then just told the truth. "Your Honor, I did all those things they say I did. I'm an alcoholic and an addict, but that's no excuse. I knew what I was doing and that it was wrong. I'm sorry for what I did." I couldn't stop the tears. "I have changed my life with God's help and the Twelve Steps, but I'm ready to face the consequences of my actions, whatever you think is fair. I'm spiritually, mentally, and physically healthy now, and I plan to come out of prison the same or even better."

The judge nodded.

I sat down, wiping away my tears.

"I will take a short recess and return with my decision."

We all stood with him, and he exited the courtroom.

Believe me, waiting for him to return was the longest ten minutes of my life.

The judge returned to the courtroom, took his place on his high bench, and said, "Mr. Eddy, please stand."

I did, and my lawyer stood beside me.

"As I thought over your case one more time in my chambers, taking into considering Mr. Brunell's testimony today along with all the letters from your friends and supporters, there can be little doubt that you have made a great change in your life. And I commend you for that. But laws have to be obeyed."

My hopes had been rising until this last sentence. Now I thought, *Oh no, he's about to drop the hammer.*

"Laws have to be obeyed," he said, "and if they are broken, there must be punishments. I sentence you to sixty months in a United States Federal Penitentiary."

Sixty months? Did I hear correctly? Just five years?

"You have ninety days to get your affairs in order. A classification officer will contact you concerning the facility you are to report to."

He banged the gavel, stood, and exited.

"Did he say five years?" I asked my lawyer.

A smile of pleasant surprise was slowly spreading across his face. "Yes," he said.

The prosecutor looked surprised too, but not in a pleasant way. It's almost unheard of in *any* court for a judge to undercut the prosecutor.

I exchanged a big smile with Larry. Yes, I was still going to prison—but five years instead of twenty-five! I knew it was a miracle, an answer to prayer.

"Let's go get a steak," Larry said.

We did, and it tasted great.

CHAPTER 14: Federal Prison

Never will I leave you; never will I forsake you –
Hebrews 13:5

In those ninety days I had before I had to turn myself in, I continued to go to Twelve Step meetings every day, to sponsor people, to take meetings into institutions—to do the basics. That's the key to staying sober—being consistent, disciplined.

I felt strong most of those ninety days, but the last couple weeks were very sad. One night my "grand sponsor" Scott—meaning he was Larry's sponsor—gave me a ride home from a meeting, and he said, "I know you're down, Robby, but keep in mind that you are not being sentenced to prison, but *called* there by God. He's got men there for you to help. He knew you could handle the job. You're going to go in there and help those men and then you're coming out!" That was a whole new way to look at what I faced, and it encouraged me (and it would prove true!).

I received a letter from the classifications officer telling me I had been assigned to the United States Federal Penitentiary in Marianna in the Florida Panhandle. My parents had moved up to Jacksonville, in that general direction, so I made plans to spend my last week of freedom with them, and then they would drive me to the prison.

I had a garage sale in which I literally put everything I owned up for sale. I didn't pack or display anything, but simply put a "Garage Sale" sign out in front of my little house, invited people in, and said, "Give me a number—name your price—and you can take whatever you want." By the end of the day, crazy enough, everything was gone—except two kitchen chairs, where Larry and I had finished reading the Big Book about a week before.

I climbed into Larry's F-250, he drove me to Jacksonville, and my parents drove me to Marianna....

... and that's how I came to be standing in the Navajo House dorm on my first day in the federal penitentiary, putting in a request for my docket sheets to prove I wasn't a chomo (child molester) or a snitch, as a fight with deadly weapons broke out a few feet away. One inmate was swinging a belt with combination locks attached at the end and the other was jabbing with a metal shank. Each of them was holding up a plastic chair as a shield. Immediately, a bunch of other prisoners rushed over, pulling out their own "homemade" weapons. I learned later that it was some kind of gang fight.

Before you knew it, the whole place was crazy. Inmates rushing to the fight, inmates running back to their cells (me included), the main metal door to the house clanging shut automatically, and—after the fight had gone on a little while—the COs busting in wearing riot gear and firing paintball guns filled with pepper spray-packed pellets at the inmates. Amid a bunch of coughing and smoking and cussing, they broke it up, put guys in cells, took others to "the shoe" (for SHU, Special Housing Unit) for solitary confinement.

All in all, it was a scary introduction to federal penitentiary life.

After the fight, they locked the whole dorm down for a week. We were stuck in our cells twenty-four hours a day. Meals were brought in to us. There were three of us in our cell, which was only six-by-eight feet with one open toilet—no privacy at all. It was literally like living in a bathroom. You can imagine what that was like with three grown men holed up in there twenty-four/seven.

The first day out of the lockdown they filed us off to the lunchroom, watching us closely, passing us through metal detectors. The lunchroom was a big octagon with long tables segregated by race, like almost everything else is in prison. Whites sat with whites, blacks with blacks, the Latinos with Latinos, etc. Even if you're not the least bit racist, you're expected to "be with your own." And there are all kinds of gangs in prison, most of them separated by race too: MS-13, Bloods and Crips, Pagans (a biker gang), Chiefs (Native Americans), and so on.

As soon as I grabbed my tray, the White Boys' shot-caller (leader) approached me. He was a musclebound skinhead plastered with tattoos. "You solid?" he said.

"What's that?"

"You a chomo or a snitch?"

"No."

"You have papers?"

"I just mailed out for them."

"I'll take your word for now," he said and led me to the White Boys' table.

Out in the rec yard it was the same thing, everybody hanging out with their races. The rec yard was a crazy place, where everything went down, because here all 1,500 inmates came together at once. It made me think of pictures of the Roman Colosseum where the gladiators used to fight, only the "spectators" here were the armed guards looking down on us from the watchtowers above the walls. It was actually a pretty nice yard, with a basketball court, a softball field, and a big track that prisoners walked around all the time. Large groups of men—again, divided by race—worked out together, doing pushups, pullups, and burpees. Staying strong for the next fight, because in prison you're either the predator or the prey.

When my docket sheets arrived, my Latino celly—a gang member covered body and face with tattoos—opened them with me in our cell. My heart was pounding, because even though I knew I wasn't a child molester or a snitch, I was thinking, *What if the papers say something wrong?* We pulled out the pages and read them together.

"You're straight, bro!" he said.

I breathed a sigh of relief.

"Hold onto these, because the White Boys will want to see them."

After the White Boys got the news, the shot-caller and a couple of his gang members came up to me on the rec yard to recruit me. All the gangs in prison want new recruits, because there is strength in numbers. So the shot-caller said, "Do you want to be with us?"

I shook my head. "No, man. I don't live like that anymore."

"What do you mean?"

"I've gotten sober and turned my life around. I don't have much time to serve, and I don't want to get in trouble and add to it."

"Then you're going to have trouble *with us!*"

"So be it," I said.

"Strap up!" he said—which means, "Tie your shoes and get ready to fight."

We were near the rec gear storeroom, where I had come to check out a basketball. We stepped inside, and one of the skinheads came at me—a tall, muscled dude with Nazi tattoos all over him. He swung and missed. I took a shot at his solar plexus and dropped him. Then I jumped on him, put my knees on his biceps, and began to pummel him. Needless to say, I tuned him up.

It was over pretty quick, and we got out of there before any COs came around.

After that, the White Boys knew I wasn't soft and laid off me the rest of my time in prison. They knew I was serious about changing my life. I still ate at their table and hung out with them—because you have to "be with your own"—but I wouldn't do any of their underworld stuff, like dealing drugs or extorting canteen money from new or weak inmates in exchange for protection.

Reaching Out

There were other guys like me, who didn't want to be part of any games but just stay out of trouble. One was Jessie Mac, who became my good friend. We worked out together, hung out together, did everything together. He was a short stocky white guy with a build like the Hulk and tattoos all over. He had been in and out of prison his whole life, struggling with drugs and alcohol—which, believe it or not, are all over federal prison. The drugs—heroin, Suboxone, weed, etc.—are "suitcased" in (i.e., hidden in certain body orifices) by visitors or returning road crews ("chain gangs"). Or they are concealed inside tennis and soccer balls that find their way over the fence. All kinds of methods. The alcohol is made just like in county jails, from fruit juice and kitchen contraband.

So I tried to help Jessie Mac out and lead by example,

because from my first week in prison I was looking for guys to help, remembering my "grand sponsor" Scott's words, "Robby, you're not being sentenced to prison, but *called* there by God." There were alcoholics and drug addicts everywhere. Ninety percent of the people in prison have a problem with drugs and alcohol and don't even realize that's the reason they're locked up.

There were no Twelve Step meetings inside, so I asked the warden and got permission to start one. We made up some flyers and passed them around and about ten guys came that first Monday night. I told my story of how the Twelve Steps and God had completely changed my life and how I had actually turned myself into prison sober.

After the meeting, a guy came up to me, and I could see the pain on his face. I could see he wanted help but was afraid to ask. I soon found out why. He was a sex offender, which puts a target on your back in prison. Your life is literally on the line every day. Same goes for anyone who hangs out with them. When I found all this out, I didn't want to help him, but I remembered something Larry said: "Robby, we don't get to pick and choose who's next. Whoever God brings us, we help."

The next day when I saw Cliff—that was his name— I told him I would sponsor him. We had to go through the Twelve Steps out in the rec yard since we lived in separate dorms. When the White Boys saw me reading the Big Book with him, they gave me dirty looks. A couple times guys asked me, "You're hanging out with a chomo. You ain't no chomo, are you?"

"You know the answer to that" is all I would say.

Working with Cliff and getting to know him gave me a compassion for guys with his sickness—because that's what I came to see that it is, a sickness. Just like alcoholism and addiction are sicknesses. That's not to equate them or excuse any of them, but just to acknowledge that they are all the result of twisted thinking. Deep down, Cliff was a good man. He didn't want to be like that.

I worked with a bunch of other men too. Most had trouble staying sober. When I complained to Larry about it on the phone, he said, "But *you're* staying sober, Robby." I knew what he meant. Even if no one listened, a big part of my own sobriety was to carry the message to them. That was Step Twelve.

Occasionally, tough guys still gave me a hard time about my Twelve Step work, but they didn't try me too much. They knew I wasn't a pushover.

A Scary Place

But prison is a scary place. I was locked up with murderers, rapists, career criminals, drug lords. It was a federal prison, with people in there for crimes against the United States, serious stuff. People were out to get each other every single day.

One time I was running around the track when I saw a group of Native Americans jump another Native American and stab him repeatedly. Another time I was in my cell brushing my teeth when I heard a *bang*. I looked out the window and saw a guy fall off the steps and another guy jump on him and hit him so hard he crushed his skull.

You never knew when someone might take a shot at you, as I would find out before my days in federal prison were over.

CHAPTER 15: "Never Seen Anything Like It"

The Lord sets prisoners free – Psalm 146:7

I had saved up as much money as I could before turning myself into prison, because I knew it was going to cost a lot to get me through a five-year sentence. It surprises some people to hear that you need money in prison, but the authorities only provide you with three thin meals a day and a few other necessities. Everything else you have to buy for yourself from the prison commissary (canteen) or go without. Things like stamps, toothbrush and toothpaste, soap, deodorant, fingernail clippers, shampoo, combs, disposable razors, washcloths, underwear, pen or pencil—things you take for granted on the outside. Plus, you can get things that add some pleasure to the long, boring days, like snacks, sodas, coffee, playing cards, etc. Not to mention, you need money to make phone calls. At Marianna the commissary was open one day a week, and we lined up outside it to buy what we needed just like from any other store.

I knew I didn't have enough money to make it through five years, so I started hustling. I was used to hustling in an illegal way—selling drugs, committing crimes—but now I was a different person and had to come up with some new way. The idea that came to me: Start a store!

You were only allowed to put $150 per week on your commissary account. So I found three guys who were indigent (didn't have any money on their accounts) and offered to pay them $10 a week if they would give me use of their accounts. Ten dollars is better than nothing, so they agreed. I filled up the rest of their accounts with my money, letting me buy three times as much stuff each week—toiletries, snacks, etc.—which I then sold to other inmates at a marked-up price, just like a retail store. Guys were always running out of items before commissary day rolled around, and they came to me for what they needed. I became the store man.

I was paid with stamps, which are prison currency. Each stamp is worth $0.25, regardless of its face value, and some stamps had been circulating around that prison for years and years. At one time I had as much as $600 in stamps hidden in a sock (they're considered contraband). If someone needed something but didn't have any stamps, I would let him have it on an IOU basis, keeping track of what he owed me on a piece of paper.

When inmates transferred from another prison, they had to leave their stamps behind, so I would give them some of my stamps, maybe as much as a couple hundred dollars' worth, in exchange for their sending, through PayPal, that amount to my mom and dad. I might also buy their shoes, because sneakers from another prison were considered unique and desirable, and sell them for a profit to someone else. On weekends, I would fill a mop bucket with ice, put sodas in it, and sell each can for $0.50.

It was crazy, but I was making money in prison. In fact, within about three months I was living pretty well for being locked up. I paid guys to clean my cell, shine my boots for visitation, and bring me eggs from the kitchen (fuel for my workouts).

I was determined to leave prison in better shape

physically, mentally, and spiritually than when I arrived. I ran five miles in the morning, another five miles at night, and worked out with Jessie Mac in-between. We didn't have any weights, so we filled laundry bags with sand for our lifting. I read the Big Book every day, and a lot of other books. And I worked through the steps with Cliff and other men.

One morning I was circling the track on my run, listening to P.O.D., a Christian rock band, on my iPod (which we were allowed to have) when the song "Alive" came on. I actually started crying as I listened to the lyrics, because, like the singer, I felt alive for the first time too. *Here I am in prison,* I thought, *but I feel the freest I have ever felt in my whole life.*

As part of my sentence, the judge had recommended me for "R-Dap," the feds' Residential Drug Abuse Program (RDAP). This program allows you to take a year off your sentence if you complete it successfully. You're housed with about fifty other guys in a separate dorm, take a bunch of classes, go to group meetings.

Ordinarily, prisoners don't enter it until they are nearing the end of their sentences. Otherwise, if they still have a lot of time to serve after completing R-Dap, they might go back in the general population and get in a fight or something and lose that year they had taken off. But for some reason, I was transferred into the program after only a few weeks at the prison. No one knew why. There was a page on the wall (it was located in the Apache House dorm) that listed the name of everyone in the program and their release date. Everyone else's release date was 2014, but mine was 2018.

It was strange, but I wasn't complaining. It wasn't a

Twelve Step program, but at least the men in it were trying to do better. We still ate and rec'd with the general population, but it got us out of a lot of the craziness.

Cliff's fifth step was a tough one, for him and for me. Step Five is to admit "to God, to ourselves, and to another human being the exact nature of our wrongs." This step was hard for me because I had to hear about all that junk from Cliff's past life, and it was hard on Cliff because he had to tell it.

But it was worth it. It seemed I could literally see the weight of the world lift off Cliff's shoulders in the process. Such a change came over his face that he looked like a completely new person.

"Never Seen Anything Like It"

One day I was lying on my bunk when I heard my caseworker's voice: "Legal mail for John Eddy." My heart dropped, because usually it's not a good thing to get legal mail. I thought, *Oh, no, they've found something else to charge me with.* I had broken the law so much that I knew it was possible.

I went out to my caseworker, a tall, silver-haired gentleman, and he walked with me back to his office. I sat down and looked up at a picture of Jesus and a cross on his wall. He pulled up a chair beside me, because legal mail had to be opened in my presence, and opened the federal court envelope. He pulled out the letter, and we saw that it was from the judge who had sentenced me. We read it together—and couldn't believe the words.

He was commuting my sentence from five years to three!

I was stunned. My caseworker was almost pale with

shock.

"This is a miracle," he said. "I've been here thirty-five years and never seen anything like it."

What he meant was that this was a motion *from the judge himself.* No one had made any appeal to him regarding my sentence, not me, not my lawyer, not the U. S. Attorney. The judge had simply taken it upon himself: Out of the blue he was reducing my sentence.

"I've never seen anything like it," the caseworker said. "And you know what else? Because you're already in the R-Dap program, you're going to get another year off your sentence. You're only going to serve two years."

Then I realized that my unexplained early transfer to the R-Dap program must have been another miracle. God had known the judge was going to do this! If I hadn't entered the program early, I wouldn't have had time to complete it and get that extra year off my sentence.

I went back to my cell and cried my eyes out with happy tears. I kept thinking about my "grand sponsor" Scott's words, "You're going to go in there, you're going to help some guys, and then you're coming out!" It was coming true. I couldn't believe all the miracles God had done for me. It was a miracle that I was alive and sober. It was a miracle that my original sentence had been just five years. It was a miracle that I went in the R-Dap program early. And now, out of the blue, my sentenced was reduced.

I realized that God had been carrying me my whole life. He had brought me through all those crazy things I had done, so he could use them to save other people's lives.

Close Call

I didn't tell a lot of people that I was getting out early, because inmates can be very jealous and do some things to get you in trouble and keep you there with them. Like crabs in a bucket, when one tries to climb out, the others will latch on and try to pull him back down.

But I did a lot of daydreaming, thinking about all the things I wanted to do with my life, including starting a new air conditioning company with Larry. I think dreaming like that is important, because the Bible says that a man without a vision perishes (Proverbs 29:18). I also dreamed about entering a CrossFit competition and taking first place.

I had a close call that almost ruined it all. About two months before I was scheduled to get out, Larry advised me to stop running the store. "You're getting out soon, and you don't need any trouble." Well, I didn't like that advice. The store helped me kill time, I liked it, and it made me money. I've learned over the years that any time I don't take my sponsor's advice, consequences tend to follow. Well, this time would be no exception.

One day I was running my store when an inmate came up to buy a bag of cookies. I gave it to him, wrote his name down, and said, "Now you owe me $1.75. Seventy-five cents for the cookies, plus the dollar you already owed me."

"No," he said, "I only owed fifty cents."

"Bro, you owed me a dollar. Trust me, I have it written down." He argued with me, and I got irritated and said, "You know what? Don't worry about it. Keep it, but don't come back here anymore!"

Later I was mopping in the showers when all of

sudden a painful *thunk!* hit me on my forehead. Blood pouring down, I looked up to see that it was my disgruntled store customer. He had attached a lock to the end of his belt and swung and hit me with it.

I glared at him with rage, and fear entered his eyes. I think he was shocked I was still standing. In fact, for some reason, I wasn't even stunned. He took off running. I can't tell you how much I wanted to chase him down and *hurt* him. To be "sucker-punched" with a deadly metal lock for fifty cents! I went back to my cell, and I was so angry and frustrated that I literally started to cry. I hit my knees. "God, please take this anger from me. I have too much to lose!"

What made things worse is that in prison, if you're hit and don't strike back, you become a target for everyone else.

"Please help me, God."

The next thing I know, I got an idea. I grabbed my beanie, pulled it down over the cut on my forehead, and went out in the rec yard. I went straight to the basketball court and said to one of the White Boys, "I need you to act like you just elbowed me in the head while we were playing." We went on the court, he bounced the ball a couple times, then pretended to elbow me. I fell down with a cry of pain and grabbed my head.

The CO came over, saw the blood, and sent me to medical—never doubting that I had been elbowed accidentally in the head. Medical bandaged me up.

That should have been the end of it, but one of the "crabs in the bucket" fired off a kite (a note) to the COs saying I had actually been injured in a fight. That got me called into the warden's office. He examined my knuckles and had me take off my shirt and looked for bruises and scratches. He didn't see any and let me go.

I breathed a sigh of relief. I came *that* close to having those three years tacked back on my sentence. I went back to my cell and got rid of my store.

CHAPTER 16: Freedom

Commit to the Lord whatever you do, and he will establish your plans – Proverbs 16:3

I t's the best feeling in the world to be getting out of prison. It's like Christmas morning times a thousand. I knew the exact day I was getting out, and when the CO walked into the dorm that morning and announced, "John Eddy, pack it all the way up. You're going home," I was ready!

Of course, all the other inmates look at you, wishing they were you. I had already said goodbye to my friends, and I was leaving most of my stuff with my celly, so I didn't have to hang around long. Then came that final walk across the grounds with the CO, the doors opened to let me *out* of the prison yard this time, and I walked into the lobby to greet my parents—in the same room where they had dropped me off two years ago. Needless to say, this was a much happier scene.

Halfway House

I had to report to a federal halfway house in Jacksonville—where my parents lived—within twenty-four hours, so I only got to spend one night at their house, and the next day my dad dropped me off at the halfway house. It was in a very poor part of town, right in the middle of the "hood," with gangs out and about. It wasn't really a house, but a big metal building lined with bunkbeds, just like the ones in prison. This halfway house wasn't a very good place to send men trying to transition back into an honest life. There were people rolling dice, drinking and doing drugs, sneaking girls in the back door, running tattoo machines, fighting—all kinds of nonsense all night long.

I immediately went up to the lady in charge and said, "I have to find a Twelve Step meeting right away. That's what will keep me sober."

"I'm sorry to hear that," she said, "but you're not going to any Twelve Step meetings. You're still in prison and you do what we tell you."

"My life is on the line," I said. "These meetings completely changed and saved me."

She just looked at me.

I didn't know what I was going to do. I knew that my sobriety depended on making meetings, but this lady couldn't care less. I found out that all the residents were given an hour and a half three times each week to go grocery shopping, so what I did was get on my phone and locate a Twelve Step meeting in a home not too far away. Then I got on the bike my dad had bought me and pedaled to that meeting; while I was there, my wonderful parents did my grocery shopping for me.

But I kept saying to the lady at the halfway house, "Listen, I need to get to West Palm Beach as soon as possible, because that's where I have the most chance for success. My sponsor is there and all the people I know in recovery, and that's where I've been doing air conditioning my whole life."

She looked at me and said, "You're never going to West Palm until you're off probation, and that's five years from now or longer, so you better just sit tight."

"Is there anything I can do?"

"You can put in for a transfer, but it's never going to happen."

I put in for the transfer and kept going about the business of working on my sobriety the best I could. To show you how God was still working, I right away at that Twelve Step meeting in someone's home met a young guy named Tom, who had a kayak rental business. He was only one day sober and needed help. I agreed to sponsor him and started working through the steps with him, and he started picking me up and giving me rides— so he was helping me out too. The crazy part is, Tom is still sober today. He's married, has a very successful business, and is completely changed. Like I said, God was working.

And believe it or not, as soon as I finished taking Tom through the steps, an official from the Federal Bureau of Prisons showed up in Jacksonville, snatched me out of the halfway house, and took me to West Palm Beach! Somehow my transfer had gone through. And I realized now why God had put me in Jacksonville: just so I could help Tom. God is good.

Hit the Ground *Sprinting*

In West Palm, I moved in with Larry's son Jerry, who was about my age and also a friend of mine. He and his wife were kind enough to rent me a room for $500 a month. I was still on house arrest, meaning I had to wear a GPS-linked monitor around my ankle, but I was free to work, and I hit the ground sprinting, never mind running.

I was going to start the air conditioning company I had dreamed about in prison. I talked Larry into being my partner. I really wanted him to be a part of it because he had always believed in me and played a big part in saving my life. He was hesitant at first, I think because he didn't want to crowd me or be pushy, but he eventually agreed and even put down the money for our first service vehicle, a $3,200 Ford van. We put out more money to letter the van professionally, registered the name Spectrum Air Conditioning with sunbiz.org, bought uniforms, and opened a bank account.

A big obstacle I faced was my lack of a contractor's license. Deep down, I had never felt smart enough to take the contractor's exam, having done so horribly in school. Plus, there was my bad criminal record. But I "happened" to meet a general contractor at Home Depot (I know now it was a God thing) who agreed to be my qualifier—a contractor under whose name I could bid for jobs and do work, a totally legit and common practice. I had to pay him $1,250 a month for the right, which was a lot of money for me at the time, but it was just something I had to do.

Next, I had to drum up some business! Larry would drive me around to house renovation sites, and I would meet GCs, subs, and project managers and take any work they would give me. Truthfully, I never had any trouble finding jobs. Part of that's because I'm very talented at AC work and have a strong work ethic, but mostly it's because God was always showing up in my life and helping me, as he still does today—it's that "unfair advantage" I'm always talking about.

I met one GC who had all kinds of work for a big company of investors that bought, renovated, and flipped houses. He gave me some work, but he would never give me any of the investors' names so I could connect with them directly. So one Friday, knowing it was payday, I followed him to a nice office building and saw him go into Prodigy Investments. I noted the address and on Monday returned in a crisp uniform and with a bunch of business cards and walked into that office just like I'd been there a million times. I introduced myself to all the project managers, underbid the competition, and cut out the middleman (the GC was pretty mad when he heard about it). I won all kinds of business.

For the next two years, I busted my tail from 7 a.m. to 11 p.m. every day, doing installs and sells during the day and running service calls at night. I didn't have a driver's license, so I would hire men to work for me and drive for me. I would teach them air conditioning and talk to them about sobriety and God. Every morning before starting my job, I hit my knees to pray, and every night I did the same. I continued to go to meetings, took meetings into institutions (various detox centers), and sponsored men. One time, when I had only $400 to my name, I spent $100 to hire a cab to take me forty-five minutes away just so I could read the Big Book with one of my sponsees. I was working as hard on sobriety and my legit business as I used to work on drinking and drugging and scamming people, and God—my Unfair Advantage—kept showing up and blessing me.

A Letter….

I eventually got off house arrest (I went into a federal halfway house in West Palm Beach to get the ankle bracelet cut off), and I found a little 750-square-foot house to rent. I saved up every penny I could, literally in a shoebox, because I was afraid the government might claim it if I put it in a bank. After a couple years I had $30,000 in that box, which I intended to use as a down payment on a house down the street.

I was single, so I spent every single moment either growing my business—we were putting new vans and crews on the road—or helping men. At one Twelve Step meeting a dude named Roman approached me and said, "Hey, man, I need to get into a detox center bad."

I said, "Look, how many times have you been to detox this year?"

"Two or three times," he said.

"Your track record stinks," I said—a line I learned from Larry. "You're going to detox with me at my house and go to meetings with me. If you need a doctor, we'll get you one."

He agreed, and we went to my place and got him through the detox.

At one point I asked him, "What do you do for a living?"

"I work in a call center."

I had to laugh. "Listen, I've got a bunch of experience with that. You quit that job immediately, because your life is on the line, and you can never stay sober working in a call center lying to people on the phone all day long."

I didn't think he would take that advice, but he did. He humbled himself, got a job washing dishes, kept working the steps, and gradually moved forward with his life. He ended up getting a job with Sprint and worked his way up the ladder and now makes six figures a year. He's been sober as of this writing for six years, owns two houses, and is about to get married. You see, when you put sobriety first and go to God for everything, the sky is the limit.

Which I certainly believed for myself, and in fact—as my business grew, I grew stronger in my sobriety, and my outreach to men continued—I could see nothing but blue skies ahead of me.

Until one day a letter arrived from the Florida Attorney General....

CHAPTER 17: Restitution and Restoration

I will restore their fortunes and have compassion on them – Jeremiah 33:26

I opened it and found a "Final Summary Judgment As To John R. Eddy" from the Circuit Court of Palm Beach County. It ordered me to pay $3,957,365.57—almost $4 million!—in restitution to victims for my part in the telemarketing scam. I was being charged $10,000 for each violation of Florida Statute 501.2075 and $15,000 for violations involving senior citizens, with some legal fees thrown in. The document said it was a "Permanent Injunction."

In one moment my "blue skies" had become a storm.

I admit I "lost my peace." I threw that letter down, cussed, swore I'd find a way to hide my money from them. How would I ever pay back $4 million? That $30,000 in my shoe box looked like little more than tip money now. How could I ever grow a business with a permanent injunction against my assets? How could I buy that house? How could I rebuild my life?

But after talking to my sponsor Larry and a night of sleep, I calmed down. I realized that now that I was sober and had turned my life over to God, I couldn't run from this. It was just something else I was going to have to man-up and face head-on—trust God and do the right thing. In one way I was just revisiting Step Nine, making amends. Here was a financial amends I had to make.

I hired a lawyer, and we started to negotiate with the attorney general. My lawyer went back and forth with them, and in the process they heard my story—how I had become sober and turned my life around—and after a couple of months they somehow agreed to demand only $88,000 from me! I was to pay it over a ten-year period at $733 a month. That was still a lot of money at that time for me, but worlds better than $4 million. Plus, my assets would be safe; they wouldn't garnish my wages or put a lien on my property as long as I paid that bill (at the time of this writing, I just made the last payment on it, years ahead of the deadline). All in all, God really worked things out for me.

Monica!

I went ahead and put that $30,000 down on that house and moved in. I was single at this time. I dated a little, and I really wanted to be in a good relationship, but I had never been very good at being tied down.

Then I met Monica!

How I met her is crazy. I used to see her around and she was beautiful, a gorgeous blend of Thai (on her mother's side) and Italian (on her father's side). Petite, and with a knockout figure. But she was always drinking and definitely an alcoholic (it takes one to know one), so I had to keep my distance. *What a shame,* I thought. *She is so beautiful.*

Well, some time went by, and I began to notice something was changing about her. Her Facebook posts were different; she was doing yoga and sharing positive sayings on her page.

I hit her up through Messenger: "Hey, I own an AC company. I do all Prodigy's air conditioning." I didn't know what else to say! I was trying to show off and making myself look lame.

"Oh yeah?" is about all she said.

"It looks like you work out," I went on to say! "I work out, and I know how hard it is to get yourself looking the way you look." *Groan. She probably thinks I'm a predator!*

Needless to say, she curbed me—acted as if I wasn't there.

I thought I'd ruined my chances, but about a month later she messaged me and asked some question about changing an AC filter. I answered her, and we started texting back and forth, and I found out that she was in the beginning steps of recovery, that she had a sponsor and was attending meetings. *That* was what was different about her. In fact, it seems she had been sort of a girl version of me, "off the chain" with drinking and drugging, in and out of jails, and at that time on house arrest because of a hit-and-run charge.

We kept texting day after day, until one day she invited me over for dinner, saying she would cook. I was really looking forward to it, but as the day approached— I stood her up!

My heart told me I shouldn't go. The reason was that I didn't want to mess up her recovery. There's an unwritten "one-year" rule in Twelve Step circles when it comes to new relationships. The first year of sobriety takes so much concentration and self-evaluation, not to mention major time commitments—meetings, counseling, working through the Big Book. At best, new relationships complicate this process; at worst, they destroy it. I didn't want to do that to her. So as bad as I wanted to see her, I didn't go.

She was pretty mad.

A few weeks later, I was thinking about her, and it

was almost as if I heard a voice say, *It's okay now.* I knew it meant it was okay to contact her now. I texted her and told her why I had stood her up, that my heart had been in the right place. We went back and forth, then she gave me her phone number and said, "Just call me."

I did, and the moment I heard her voice (this was the first time we had spoken) I fell in love with her! I can't explain it, but I really did. I knew she was the one.

She invited me over for dinner again, and this time I went! The dinner was amazing—ribeye and sweet potato. She was amazing—so beautiful and sweet. And long-story-short, we've been together ever since. We're married now, with four beautiful children, two awesome boys that Monica brought into the marriage with her and another boy and a baby girl who have been born to us since. We are blessed!

Having children has helped me understand how much God loves us. I love my children unconditionally and would do anything in the world for them and want them to have the best. I realize now that that is how God feels about us, only multiplied a million times over! Because he is perfect love, not a sinful, fallible man. As humans, we have to try hard to be good people, but God is good in his very nature. He loves us completely. He wants us to have our hearts' desires, to have great lives, be good people. We're his children.

And he's given me the wife of my dreams in Monica, my "twin flame," my best friend. She has become a girl version of me in another way now: She goes hard at her sobriety, works hard to rescue women who need God and the Twelve Steps, sponsors women, and leads meetings. She is my love, my partner, woven from the rib nearest my heart (Genesis 2:21-22).

Driver's License

Before I went to prison, I had received a letter from the DMV telling me I had lost my driver's license "for the remainder of my life." (What's the saying, "When it rains, it pours"?) At the time I didn't do anything about it, figuring it was the least of my worries compared to the prison sentence hanging over my head. But now that I was trying to grow a business and rebuild my life, catching rides from my employees or Ubering all over was getting old. So I hired *another* lawyer to see if I could get it back.

The first thing I had to do was go before a judge and pay a bunch of judgments—old tickets and court fees—all of which came to $20,000! Then I had to make my appeal to the DMV board, because no one—no judge or anyone—can restore your license except the DMV. I asked friends and people who knew me from Twelve Step groups to write letters of recommendation for me, then I went before the board with my lawyer.

It was by teleconference, four or five people on the other end of the line in Tallahassee, their leader a woman whose stern voice made it clear what she thought of my chances.

"This meeting is being recorded, Mr. Eddy," she said.

There were various preliminaries—a rehashing of my record, a passing mention of my letters of recommendation, my lawyer's spiel—then it was my turn to speak. I just spoke from my heart, telling my story, being completely transparent. I told them how alcoholism and addiction had ravaged my life, but how God and the Twelve Steps had changed it. I told them how I was trying to rebuild my life. I spoke for about ten or fifteen minutes, and they listened quietly.

When I was finished, their leader said, "There's someone upstairs looking out for you." Her tone was no longer harsh. "I'm very proud of you."

They all agreed and encouraged me to keep doing what I was doing.

Then they said they wanted to take a break to talk among themselves. My lawyer and I waited. When they came back on the speakerphone, the lady said they had voted to restore my license! My lawyer and I were shocked; we weren't expecting any decision on the spot.

"There will be a five-year probation period," the leader said, "in which you'll have to install—and pay for—a breathalyzer in your vehicle."

That didn't bother me at all. My license, which had been revoked *for the remainder of my life*, had just been restored to me! I walked out of there floating on air.

Dreams

Step by step God was restoring my life and granting me the daydreams I had envisioned in prison. The growing business. A beautiful wife and family. My driver's license. And many little things, like winning a CrossFit competition and buying (after my license was restored) a sweet black GMC Yukon Denali!

One of the main things I had dreamed about in prison was to one day be able to walk back in *as a free man* and bring the Twelve Steps to men. I didn't know how that would be possible with my record. For example, the first two questions on the Florida Department of Corrections Volunteer Application are "Have you ever been arrested on a misdemeanor or felony charge?" and "Have you ever been convicted on a misdemeanor or felony charge?" Of course, my arrest record ran for pages.

But I filled out the applications, again asked people to write letters of recommendation for me, wrote my own letter, etc., and believe it or not, they approved me. First, the state prisons, then the Palm Beach County Jail, where I had been incarcerated almost fifty separate times since the age of seventeen. It was unbelievable. Soon Larry and I were taking meetings behind bars three times a week.

And the men listened. You see, I remember hearing cops, parents, psychiatrists—everybody—telling me over and over again my whole life to get it together, to change my ways. *But they didn't have the disease, so it* went in one ear and out the other. But when another man comes up to you, a man *who has been there* and made it through alive, you listen. You know there's hope. *If he can change, so can I!* I've seen so many people—not only in prison, but people I grew up with, people I just happen to meet—turn their lives around because they hear my story. It's pretty amazing. It's all God's doing.

There was one more dream that I really considered beyond my reach: getting my contractor's license. I had owned my AC company for a few years now but was still paying the qualifier $1,250 each month to work under his license. People would say, "You should just take the contractor's exam, Robby, get your own license," but I didn't think I was book-smart enough to do it. That SLD label from my school days—"Slow Learning Disability"—still hovered over me like a cloud.

But I was a different person now, and I had seen so many miracles....

I went ahead and bought the books, nineteen of them!

and started studying. For a year, I hit the books every day. I still worked at my AC business fulltime, but each day I would stop for an hour at one of the different libraries around Palm Beach County and study. It was *tough*.

When the day of the test came, I drove down to Boynton Beach and sat with a bunch of other people in cubicles around a big room and took the test. It took hours. I was trying for the most advanced license I could get, so I would be able to do any size job, commercial or residential, and the test literally took all day.

When I was finished, I walked up to the computer screen that told whether you had passed or failed....

... and I had failed.

By one question!

I was disappointed but no way was I giving up. I hit the books for another six months, drove down to Boynton Beach, and took it again.

Again, it took all day. The contractor's test is broken into two parts, and this first half of the test, which I was taking that day, is the "trade knowledge" part, with all kinds of technical questions about load and energy calculations, reading blueprints, knowing building codes, etc., and is very hard.

I submitted my answers, walked up to the computer to see my results, and could barely believe my eyes....

... I had passed!

The SLD kid had just passed a test that seventy-five percent of the people who take it fail. I went into the restroom in tears, hit my knees, and thanked God.

I still had another half of the test to take, focusing on OSHA policies, accounting standards, and various laws. I studied for another six months, drove down to Boynton

Beach, took the test, and this time passed on the first try. Again, I was in tears. It's hard to express how much it meant to me.

There remained one more *high* hoop to jump through to get my license. I had to appear in person before the Florida Construction Industry Licensing Board in Tallahassee. Like all applicants, I would have to answer all the technical and industry questions they asked me. *Unlike* other applicants, I would have to explain my criminal record. More than one person said to me, "Yeah, you passed the test, but they're never going to give you a contractor's license with all those arrests."

Larry made the trip to Tallahassee with me. The board met on the top floor of a huge hotel, in a ballroom converted into a hearing room for the day. The board members, long-time contractors of various industries— air conditioning, electrical, plumbing, and so on—sat around a big square table in the middle of the floor, with the applicants, one at a time, called to sit at the table with them and answer questions. Another applicant was getting grilled when I arrived.

As I sat waiting my turn, I was so nervous I was sick to my stomach. Out of nowhere this tall, slim cowboy with long hair and a salt-and-pepper goatee walked up to me. "Don't worry, man," he said, "Jesus has your back." A little bit later he came back up to me and handed me a piece of paper with a phone number on it. "I want you to do me a favor, son. After you get that license, because I know you will, call me and let me know." I didn't know him from Adam, but the way he talked to me calmed me down quite a bit.

Then they called my name. I went to the table and sat down. They had my paperwork in front of them, which included the information about my criminal record, and they looked at me closely—at least I imagined they did. They started off with technical questions, which tripped me up, because I was expecting to be asked about my record, and I could barely talk at first, stuttering out my answers.

Then came the questions about my criminal past. I just answered from the heart, like I always do. I told them how much I had messed up my life in the past and how much I had changed. I told them how I pray every day, go to meetings every day, sponsor men, and take the Twelve Steps back into the prisons and jails. Just my story, as transparently as possible.

They listened to every word.

Then they looked at each other and one of them suddenly said, "All in favor?"

"Aye!" they all answered.

I sat there stunned, so shocked I could barely think. Just like that I had my contractor's license! My Certified Air-Conditioning Contractor's License. I felt lightheaded.

I got up and walked over to Larry, and he was crying happy tears for me.

When we got in the truck, I took out my phone and texted the cowboy: "I got approved."

"God is great," he texted back.

Believe it or not, I was about to experience just *how* great.

CHAPTER 18: Jesus Calling

Everyone who calls on the name of the Lord will be saved – Romans 10:13

Monica and I were living in a nice new house by now. That little 800-square-foot house, which I had put that $30,000 down on to buy, was no place to raise a family. Not only was it small, it was in a bad neighborhood.

Selling it and moving into a new place involved a few more miracles. In the first place, we were able to get $185,000 for it, though I had paid only $100,000 to buy it and nothing in our area was selling at the time. But for some reason, suddenly three buyers wanted it, and a bidding war broke out! So we got $185,000 for it.

Of course, now we had to find a new place to live. Monica saw a house she loved, a large white home with stately columns and wide, regal steps leading up to the front door. But it was going for $465,000.

"No way, babe," I had to say. "Maybe someday."

"Guess who owns it? Prodigy Investments."

"What?!" I said.

By now I'd been doing Prodigy's AC work for years, and so I got on the line with Chris Graeve, one of the owners, and told him we really wanted that house. He said, "Come by the office, and we'll talk." He ended up selling us that beautiful house for $390,000, with a $10,000 roof credit thrown in.

I don't know why Chris gave us such a great deal, unless it was just because it was a part of God's plan for us, because the contractor who came out to do the roof would play a big role in my life. He was Ed Campany (of Campany Roofing Maintenance) and he was a very prosperous entrepreneur, with a bunch of trucks on the road and thousands of successful jobs to his credit. Whenever I meet someone like him, I ask them how they became so successful, so I can learn from them. So I picked Ed's brain too, and I could tell there was something special about him.

Early one morning, when I was praying and reading my Twelve Step reflections, I got this text from him:

"Robby, what I didn't tell you is how I really grew my business. I use it as a ministry. Every month I pick someone to bless with a roof. Sometimes a complete roof and sometimes a partial roof project. Last year I gave away over $440,000 in roofing. Some of these people really need help, some are young people just starting to dream about their future. There is nothing more rewarding than to give freely the gift that you were given to provide for your family.

"Robby, I'm just a dumb roofer. I was raised on welfare. I have an eleventh-grade education, and I battled drug addiction for decades. But this year we will do over $25 million dollars of business. I just sent $27,000 to Romania to install a new roof. And I can't wait for the next person to show up that needs my help. Robby, God gave you a gift of knowledge in the AC area. Use your gift as a gift from time to time and watch your business grow and grow."

He went on to say:

"Do you see what time I'm sending this? I am up praying for my wife. If I can make her world special, she will make me the king of her world. When our brides start getting a little older, that is when their real beauty shines through. Their love, support, and encouragement. Enjoy, my friend."

I was blown away by what I read, and it would change my life forever, starting with my first service call that morning. It was for a lady in a two-story house in Loxahatchee, whose upstairs AC unit had been broken for two years and whose downstairs unit had given out that morning. It seemed like these were real good people—the house was clean, little kids were running around—who had fallen on some hard times. Her husband may have been an electrician, because there were neat rolls of wire and tools here and there. I looked at the AC units and told her, "They aren't worth fixing. They're both in bad shape."

"We just can't afford to change them now. Can you do anything with them at all?"

I thought of Ed's text.

"I'll have somebody out here at nine on Monday morning to take care of it."

On Monday I sent my crew out there with two brand-new units to install, but told them, "Don't charge her." Later that day I was sitting in my truck at another job, doing paperwork, when she texted me. In the text she was thanking me like crazy, saying she couldn't believe I had given them two brand-new air conditioners. Then my phone rang, and it was her, thanking me some more, crying. "I'll tell *everybody* about your company!" she said. "Oh, thank you so much!"

It was a great feeling. It woke something up inside me.

The Missing Piece

So many things had fallen into place for me—the wife of my dreams, our amazing children, my contractor's license, taking meetings into the prisons....

But I always felt like something was missing somehow. I was happy, and life was great, but sometimes I would wake up with a little bit of fear, like I used to when I was drinking and drugging. I'd be worried and anxious for no reason, because life was great. It was crazy. And I was still struggling with my anger quite a bit, losing my temper and snapping at people, then afterward feeling horrible. I even went to a therapist for help.

One morning I happened to notice Monica's book, *Jesus Calling,* lying on the couch. Monica was already a Christian, but strange as it may sound, considering that my whole sobriety was a miracle of God, not to mention all the other miracles he had performed for me, I wanted nothing to do with that "religious stuff." If anybody mentioned Jesus or the Bible to me, I just shut them down immediately. But this morning, as I looked at that *Jesus Calling* book, I was interested.

Go ahead, pick it up and read it, a calm voice seemed to whisper to me.

Don't read that! another kind of voice whispered. *It's all bull.*

I picked it up and started reading:

"Come to Me with a teachable spirit, eager to be changed. A close walk with Me is a life of continual newness. Do not cling to old ways as you step into a new year. Instead, seek My Face with an open mind, knowing that your journey with Me involves being transformed by the renewing of your mind. As you focus your thoughts on Me, be aware that I am fully attentive to you. I see you with a steady eye because My attention span is infinite. I know and understand you completely; My thoughts embrace you in everlasting love. I also know the plans I have for you: plans to prosper you and not to harm you, plans to give you hope and a future. Give yourself fully to this adventure of increasing attentiveness to My Presence."

It hit me between the eyes. I felt like God was speaking directly to me. I thought about the times I had refused to go to church with Monica and had even held her back. I still wasn't interested in going to church, but I liked what I was reading, so I kept reading a portion of that book every morning for about six months. Finally, one day I said in my heart, *Maybe I should go to church just to support my wife.*

We went to Christ Fellowship, a megachurch with about 28,000 members and multiple locations around southern Florida. That first time I went I was completely thrown off. I saw some guy with a gold chain or bright smile and thought, *Yeah, but I wonder how you live during the week.* (I was just looking for things to criticize.) They talked a little bit about money and passed around the offering baskets, and I thought, *See, all they care about is money.* I shut down and didn't even pay attention to the sermon.

When we were walking in the parking lot after church, I was already thinking, *I'll never come back here again.* Then some words from the Big Book came to my mind: *Don't miss the beauty of the forest because of the ugliness of some its trees.* Those words are from a section of the Big Book that discusses believing in a Power greater than yourself. I felt like they had been whispered to me by that same calm voice that had told me to pick up the *Jesus Calling* book.

Well, maybe I'll come back again, I thought.

The next weekend I was there with Monica again. This Sunday there was a guest speaker, a minister from Texas named Robert Morris, who had written a book called *Beyond Blessed.* He was preaching about tithing, the Biblical practice of giving the first ten percent of your income to God.

Money again!

I couldn't believe it. I was squirming in my seat. This guy was talking about giving ten percent of my money to the church.

But reminded not to "miss the beauty of the forest," I listened. I didn't know what to make of his teaching about tithing—I'd never heard of it before—but he seemed sincere, like he really cared about his audience. At one point he appealed tearfully, "Please listen to me. Only about ten percent of Christians actually tithe. If you're not one of them, you have no idea of the blessings you're missing. Not only financially, but the freedom you will have in your relationship with God is beyond your wildest dreams." Then it dawned on me that he wasn't even from this church. What did he care if money came in or not? *He must really mean what he is saying.*

Convinced he was genuine, I listened closely to what he said about Jesus, and I saw that I had a messed-up view of him. I thought he was just a good man who lived a long time ago. It had never clicked with me that he was the Son of God whose death on the cross had taken the penalty for my sins. I knew all about paying a penalty for your wrongs—federal prison!—and to think that Jesus had done that for me got to me. At the end of his sermon, when he asked if anyone wanted to accept Jesus, I raised my hand and repeated the prayer after him:

"Dear Lord Jesus, I admit that I'm a sinner and need your forgiveness. Thank you for dying in my place on the cross and coming back to life to live in me. Please forgive my sins and change my heart. I accept you as my Lord and Savior. Amen."

Right away I felt a new peace. It was hard to believe that I had never done this before, since God had been my constant Companion and Helper since that night I hit my knees beside my bunk in the Stockade and he had taken away my obsession to drink and drug. But the Bible says the devil keeps a veil over people's eyes to keep them from seeing the glory and truth of Jesus (2 Corinthians 4:3-6).

Leaving church that day, it was awesome to know that I had a home waiting for me in Heaven now. I had already cleaned up most of my life, morally speaking, through following the Twelve Step process, so most of my changes after accepting Jesus were internal. I stopped worrying all the time. I wasn't afraid of anything anymore. I got a better hold on my temper (when you're at peace with yourself, it's hard to be mad at others). And the joy! When you know that eternal life awaits you, every day is like a Friday! There's nothing like it.

Like everything else I've done in my life, I went all-in on being a Christian too. I still went hard at my sobriety—going to meetings every day, sponsoring men, taking meetings into institutions—and I always will. But now I follow Jesus too. Every morning I get up before dawn, like Jesus did (Mark 1:35), to pray to my Heavenly Father. I read the Bible along with my Twelve Steps reflections. I walk into my bedroom and pray over my wife, then into my kids' rooms and pray over them. As I head out into my day, I ask God to put someone in my path that I can bless—with the Twelve Steps, with the good news about Jesus, with my business. I've become a "fisher of men" (Matthew 4:19), not only to alcoholics and addicts, but to those who need Jesus.

Overflowing Blessing

You'll never guess what else I started to do....
Tithe!

Believe it or not, I made the decision to do it that same day I accepted Jesus. After the sermon that day, I picked up an offering envelope to put a little cash in it to ease my conscience when I saw this Bible verse printed on the back of the envelope:

> *"Bring all the tithes into the storehouse so there will be enough food in my Temple. If you do," says the Lord of Heaven's Armies, "I will open the windows of heaven for you. I will pour out a blessing so great you won't have enough room to take it in! Try it! Put me to the test!"* (Malachi 3:10, NLT)

I knew God was talking to me. But it was really hard to start tithing. I would think, *This is like a car payment.* Plus, I needed that money for the mortgage, the kids, the restitution payment, etc., and I had worked so hard for that money. It didn't help that when I asked other Christians if they tithed, most of them said, "No, because we don't have to, we're under grace."

So I called up Ed, the roofer, to ask his opinion.

"Take a look at the lives of those who don't tithe, Robby," he said. "Are they doing as well as they could be?"

"No, they don't seem to be doing that well. Just getting by."

"Because they're not taking advantage of God's promises. It's not that we *have* to tithe. We *get* to tithe."

As soon as I started to tithe, it was amazing. Business started flooding in. I went from having three trucks on the road to ten. I soon had fifteen guys working for me—me, a convicted felon, who wasn't even supposed to be employable himself. My income literally tripled. I had done what that verse said to do, put God *"to the test,"* and God had done what he said he would do: *"pour out a blessing so great you won't have enough room to take it in!"*

I remember how I used to think, back before I got sober, that I had ruined my chances for a good life. *My life is going to stink even if I do get sober,* I thought. *No driver's license. A record a mile long. Who's going to hire me? How am I ever going to have anything? I'm going to be poor and broke my whole life.* Now I have to pinch myself on almost a daily basis. I'm blessed beyond belief. A thriving business, a prosperous family life, and I've travelled all over—to Italy for my honeymoon, to Costa Rica, to Cuba three years in a row just to drink the coffee! All of this for a guy who could have been dead in a gutter many times. When you put God first place, the sky's the limit!

CHAPTER 19: The Unfair Advantage

For I can do everything through Christ, who gives me strength – Philippians 4:13 (NLT)

Wow! I've had a crazy life story, I know. One many people wouldn't even believe. It's been crazy bad—addiction, overdoses, crime, death threats, and incarceration. It's become crazy good—sobriety, prosperity, a beautiful family, and a miraculous walk with God.

The reason I wrote this book is to let everyone know that they can get in on the crazy good part. Everyone has the same opportunity. I'm nobody special. I just hit rock bottom in my life and turned to God and the Twelve Steps. Anyone can do it.

Early in my journey through the Twelve Steps, my sponsor Larry sat me down with the Big Book and said, "Robby, with this book, the Twelve Steps, and God, you will have an unfair advantage in life. You will conquer addiction. You will help others. You will succeed everywhere you go." I have found Larry's words to be true!

At this writing, I have been sober ten years. Over those years, as I've told my story, people kept telling me, "You need to write a book," and I kept telling them, "Yeah sure, one day. One day." But it seemed like one thing or another kept getting in the way. Looking back, I realize it was God who had it on hold—because my story wasn't complete yet. But after I accepted Jesus into my heart, after I met in a personal way the God who had set me free from alcoholism and addiction, it clicked. *It's time to write that book*, a voice said in my heart. *Not for money or fame, but to save lives. Like yours was saved.*

That's the reason this book found its way into your hands—to save you or someone you know. If you have the disease—if you're struggling with the beast of alcoholism or addiction—get to a Twelve Steps meeting immediately. Get a sponsor. Start working the steps. Because the truth is, it's either "Get busy living or get busy dying." Your life *is* on the line. If you're not sure about the "God thing," that's okay too. When I knelt beside that bunk in the Stockade and prayed for help, I didn't even know if I believed in God. Just start where you are; he'll meet you there. He wants to be your Unfair Advantage too.

- Robby

Testimonies

Declare the praises of him who called you out of darkness into his wonderful light – 1 Peter 2:9

Kevin

My name is Kevin and I'm an alcoholic and addict. I was raised in Lake Park, Florida, and went to local schools. I was raised from a good family with strong values. My father never graduated high school but after a Navy stint took up tool design and excelled. From this accomplishment he was hired by Pratt and Whitney and was transferred to West Palm in 1957. He worked his way up to the top of management and retired at 55 years old.

My mother became ill with multiple sclerosis at an early age of 22 and after several years my father chose to put her in a nursing home. I think my resentment for my father came when this happened. I kind of understood but I really didn't. This was when a lot of my troubles began. Running away from home, getting into little amounts of boyish trouble. Then I graduated to picking up drinking and drugs at the age of 13 or 14. It really never stopped from that day on. I was always deceiving my parents, lie after lie. I played baseball and football from Pee Wee Football and Little League Baseball all through junior high and high school. I seemed to always make the first squad.

But alcohol and drugs were still in my life. I remember taking acid before football practice in my senior year, but there were plenty of other times this happened.

My criminal career really started when I was 18. I got the bright idea to smuggle weed from Jamaica and coming through customs they picked me out of three of us that went. I remember calling my father and once again it was hard. He hired me a good attorney and under the youth offenders act once I served my time in federal custody I would be on my own recognizance.

I still didn't quit. I started selling drugs from that time on until I really hit it big and was arrested for trafficking in cocaine and trafficking in marijuana and was part of a large scale smuggling operation. I'm leaving a lot of things out, criminal stuff.... After being arrested in 1981, we hired three attorneys, one for each of us charged, and I was looking at 30 years of time in prison. Fortunately, like my father used to say, I "was born with a golden horseshoe in my pocket." I received four months in the Stockade and five years probation.

I quit selling drugs but never stopped drinking and drugging. I ended up violating probation, and again my father came to the rescue and posted a $20,000 bond. My problem was lifted. I started my first real job at 27 years old. I got married and had two kids from my marriage but continued to drink and drug. This eventually led to divorce along with three DUIs, one boating under the influence, drug possession, detoxes, hospitalizations. I never thought I had a problem—really.

But this last time in the hospital on my death bed, I really believe that God said to me, "This is enough. I need you for other uses," and that day I began my journey of recovery. After a week of going to AA, a man came into my life through God's will and became my sponsor. His name is Robby, and I am blessed that he has spent the time with me, and along with God's inspiration has been leading me through this journey, and I feel blessed every day I wake up sober with no obsession of a drink or drug. It really is a miracle. I had nothing to do with it, it's God's plan for me that is making this happen. Today I am almost eight months sober, chairing meetings, bringing AA meetings to detoxes and sponsoring men.

Jonathan

My name is Jonathan and I'm currently sitting on my bunk incarcerated in a Florida Department of Corrections work release center. I'm finishing up a 5-year sentence. I was asked by my brother in Christ that wrote this book to write a short testimony that he was going to include in this book. I was more than happy to do that.

My story is very similar to his. Alcohol and drug addiction destroyed my life. My life was so dark and depressing I was on the verge of death and welcomed the idea. I was so lost and didn't have the first idea of how to fix what was wrong. There was no consequence that could stop me. Alcoholism was trying to kill me and I was doing everything in my power to help make that happen. I was sent to prison again and was still using. I was doing what 95% of all the inmates in institutions do, drinking and drugging, just doing what I could not to face the reality of what my life was and had become. The further I got in my alcoholism and drug addiction the more I wanted to drink and drug so I didn't have to face reality.

Then one day I was detoxing in my cell on this sentence and had these thoughts that I just wanted to stop. I had a little experience with AA when I was on the street, in and out of treatment centers, with no results. I later would learn that was because I didn't put into action what I was hearing, but I would just go through the motions. Two guys brought a meeting into the institution I was in and I started attending those meetings and took every one of their suggestions seriously this time. I did exactly what was suggested to me. I had another man in blues take me through the steps and then I took another man through the steps myself. Robby was one of those guys that brought that meeting into the institution and was giving those suggestions. I now know God used Robby to carry that message to me because God knew that he was the one to get that message across to me.

So AA got me on a spiritual path that prepared me for what God really had in store for me. I would not be sober today if it wasn't for AA and I know I cannot stay sober without it. I know God uses certain people to carry the message of Jesus Christ to certain people because the way Jesus Christ was brought to me by Robby was different than the way I'd heard it before. I know today that it really wasn't Robby, it was God the whole time. I accepted Jesus Christ into my heart on January 1st at 1:04 p.m. while I was working. Robby asked me, "Have you been born again?" I said, "Not yet." Robby said, "Very easy, bro. Pray this prayer: Dear Lord Jesus, I know that I am a sinner, and I ask for Your forgiveness. I believe You died for my sins and rose from the dead. I turn from my sins and invite You to come into my heart and life. I want to trust and follow You as my Lord and Savior." I prayed that and my life has never been the same since that day. That was the greatest day of my life. I pray and meditate on God's word every morning and I have found the answers to all my problems in his word.

Robby told me a story about how he was in church one time at the beginning of his walk with Christ and how he saw an envelope with the verse Malachi 3:10 on it: "Bring the whole tithe into the storehouse, that there may be food in my house. Test me in this, says the Lord Almighty, and see if I will not throw open the floodgates of heaven and pour out so much blessing that there will not be room enough to store it." And he started tithing and his experience was countless blessings. So I started tithing right away. Jesus Christ had made such an impact in my life that I didn't want to miss out on any of his blessings. I never started tithing with the expectation of getting money in return. It was never about money. It was about faith, it helps my faith grow so much stronger.

I used to think I was tough and had a lot of ego and pride issues, especially with my history of being in and out of prison, but when I got saved and started reading about my favorite apostle, Paul, I realized how tough I really wasn't. God took someone that was killing Christians (Paul) and turned him into a disciple to carry the message of Jesus Christ. God had him do the very thing that he used to be killing people for, preaching the message of Jesus. If that doesn't demonstrate the power of Jesus Christ, I don't know what does. Oh wait, there's more: Paul was beaten, stoned, and lashed numerous times because of his faith. That helped me become humble.

I wouldn't change anything. They say if you want to make God smile, tell him your plans. I tell Jesus everything today. I try to make him smile as much as I can. My spirituality is so strong today because Jesus Christ used another man to bring me into the light. "Don't let too much light in at the beginning, because you don't want it to blind you" was advice that was given to me. I'm new in my walk with Christ, but according to a story I read in the Bible about a vineyard owner, "So the last will be first, and the first will be last" (Matthew 20:16). The parable means that even those who are converted to Christianity late in life earn equal rewards along with those converted early, and that people who were converted early in life need not feel jealous of those later converts. Today my king is Jesus Christ. I used to wonder if I would ever have a spiritual experience, but I have had so many God moments since I've been saved that I no longer question myself about that today. I've had moments that out of nowhere I will think about God and my eyes will literally start watering. Knowing God has my back, I just know everything is going to be alright. If you haven't accepted Jesus Christ into your heart as your Lord and Savior, I strongly recommend it. Like Robby said, "It's very easy." Pray this: "Dear Lord Jesus, I know that I am a sinner, and I ask for Your forgiveness. I believe You died for my sins and rose from the dead. I turn from my sins and invite You to come into my heart and life. I want to trust and follow You as my Lord and Savior."

Deb

From a very early age, I always knew there was a God. I do not really know how I knew but I just knew.

Growing up with a family history rooted in alcoholism—my parents were adult children of alcoholics—and being a victim of sexual abuse, emotional "enmeshment," and neglect, it is perhaps not surprising that I wound up an alcoholic.

In 1990, through Al-Anon (a recovery program for the families and friends of alcoholics), I was introduced to the Twelve Steps and got "sober." I attended meetings for four years, worked with a sponsor, and completed my steps. But in 1993 I had a spiritual awakening and, assuming I did not need the Twelve Steps anymore, I walked away from my program and my recovery; I know now it was a wrong decision.

As the years passed, I gradually returned to my "isms" one by one, and in 2008 I relapsed into my alcoholism. A few months later, knowing I needed to stop, I did; but I did not return to the Twelve Steps because—Hey, I had just stopped drinking on my own, so I wasn't an alcoholic, right?

Wrong.

And the saddest part of my story is that I always thought it was the other people in my life who had the problems, because I was "perfect" and had it all together. After all, I could stop and had gone years without picking up a substance. The trouble was that I picked up other addictions instead: workaholism, perfectionism, over-done caretaking, an eating disorder, and love or sex addiction. But denial ran very deep in my life, and it was not until March of 2020 when my life had fallen apart so much that I told my husband of over 30 years that our marriage was over, not because of my alcoholism and addictions, but because of his. Like I said my denial ran deep.

I entered inpatient treatment on March 1st, 2020, and I found the Twelve Steps once again, but this time I had God in my life, and I discovered that the life I had lived before was nothing like the kind of life I was going to have with my God. The Twelve Steps have connected my dots and with the daily help of my God I have an awareness of myself like I never had. I no longer must be in control. I can feel what I am experiencing and not have to run. I have a peace and serenity I never thought I could possess. Because of God and the Twelve Step program, my life has been saved, and I no longer need to run and hide behind alcohol or any of my addictions.

Ed

I, Edward Grant Campany, was raised by a single mom on welfare. My entire family had major drinking and drugging problems (even my grandmother). As a child, I stuttered badly. For some reason, all the kids and some of my older family members thought it was funny to pick on me. So I had serious self-esteem issues from a very young age.

Nobody ever showed interest in me or encouraged me as a child, or even into my adult years. I never had direction or hope, and I planned on being a good-for-nothing welfare rat just like folks called me. Moreover, I had become a good drunken drug addict like the family I grew up with. From the earliest I can remember and up until the age of 38, nobody—man, woman, or child—ever encouraged me or helped me better myself.

Then a man came along, and he started to encourage me and speak life into me, telling me I could be anything I wanted to be. Better yet, he said, "God wants you to prosper, and he wants you to live abundantly." This man was my first pastor. I grabbed hold of what he said, and I began to believe all of God's promises, better yet I began to receive these promises. My pastor taught me about tithing, giving, sowing and reaping, and the importance of following God's financial principles.

171

This totally changed our lives. I went from being raised on welfare with no hope to a good life, and then to my wife and I owning a roofing company. We opened this company with $3,000, and I had to borrow a pickup truck for two months. We followed God's financial principles. We studied these principles and then we applied them to our personal lives and to our businesses. We experienced miracle after miracle after miracle. Maybe one day we will write a book about all of them.

I will share this one big miracle. We started with no jobs, no money, no vehicles, no equipment, and no real estate—personal or business real estate. Today we have over 250 employees, over 60 commercial vehicles, too many pieces of equipment to count, over $7.4 million in business real estate, over $1 million in personal real estate, and we expect to do between $42 million and $48 million in revenue this year (2021). Moreover, I was cured of Hepatitis C, survived a triple bypass, and I was delivered from drugs and alcohol. As I stated, the list of miracles could go on and on and on....

Now that I have shared the amazing life of living in God's promises and following God's financial principles, I also need to share that even with all those miracles and God's wonders, I was not able to hold off the grip of addiction. Early on in my Christian walk, I had experienced what is known as "deliverance," which basically sets you free from drugs, alcohol, and addictions. I honestly lived a clean and sober life for a little over 10 years. But the problem was, I had not educated myself on this terrible disease and the pitfalls of not working a recovery program. I relapsed in late spring of 2001. I continued to relapse for the next 20 years.

Finally, in June 2020, my therapist informed me (while I sat in my second treatment center of the year) that she would no longer be able to help me. She explained that she had done all she knew to do and none of it stopped me from relapse. She then told me that if I agreed to get a sponsor, do 90 meetings in 90 days, and work the Twelve Steps of AA, she would continue to help me. She told me she knew this would help me and pointed out that we had tried everything else, so why not give this a try?

To be honest, I had always said that I would "never" do AA or get a sponsor. But God had other plans for me. My friend Robby Eddy also called me while I was in treatment. He called to encourage me and ask me a few questions about God and business. I was too ashamed to let Robby know I was in a treatment center. A couple weeks later, I got out of treatment and Robby called me again. This time God gave me the grace and the courage to share with Robby how desperate I was. Robby dropped everything that day to take me to an AA meeting. To make a long story short, the miracle of "never" happened that day. I received a white chip, the chip of surrender. Robby became my sponsor and my journey in AA began.

I am arming myself with facts. Robby told me I have an unfair advantage, and you know what? I believe him. I realize it has been only eight months since my last relapse, but something is very different this time. I am accountable to my sponsor, my home group, the institution I take an AA meeting into, my sponsor group, my family, and myself.

Words will never begin to express my love and appreciation for Robby and all he has done for me and my family. Robby Eddy, I love you, buddy!

Sincerely,
Eddie Campany

Monica

When I came to the point of surrender, I was completely broken. For years I was searching for things and experiences to fill this void inside of me. I was always after the next experience or the next "cure all" for my emptiness. I managed to rake in a federal arrest, a drug trafficking arrest, and my children being taken by the state due to my drug and alcohol addiction.

When I finally hit rock bottom, I came to the realization that I had but two options—get help or die. I remember hitting my knees and having that moment of total surrender. I didn't pray a long, drawn-out prayer, I just simply asked for help because I couldn't do it on my own anymore. Help came in the form of sponsorship with a sponsor from my Twelve Step program.

I got sober in pretty rough conditions, facing up to twenty years in prison. I had to face the battle of confronting my chaotic life head on. I had serious consequences from my drinking and drugging coming in from all directions. During my entire open case, I continued to persevere and work my Twelve Steps. Everything on the outside was showing me that I was going to prison. The victim of my last crime was not accepting my sincere apology and the prosecutor on my case was not letting up on her heavy recommendation for prison time. In spite of all my unfavorable exterior

174

circumstances, I chose to trust God. By the time I finished my steps, I began to feel a sense of purpose in life, a sense of self-worth and self-love. That void I was trying to fill in my active addiction was a void only the presence of God could fill. It took facing my checkered past, putting pen to paper to take a look at my resentments, and setting right my wrongs in the form of making amends.

My most important purpose in this life is to help the next alcoholic/addict that is suffering from the disease of addiction. I'm now six years sober and have a life beyond my wildest dreams. I have four beautiful children and am married to my best friend who completes me. I now have full custody of a child that was taken from me eight years ago. I am the mother I always dreamed of being. I am a licensed General Contractor and own a construction company. I have been convicted of two felonies and should amount to nothing according to society. I have risen above my bondage and have been set free by the power of Jesus and the Twelve Steps.

My husband (Robby, the author of this book) and I are on this journey of life together. We share the same calling in life—to pull others back from the gates of death. Christ who abides in us both is the cement which binds us. To be equally yoked with your spouse and truly know the fundamentals of a Kingdom marriage is life changing. I am so grateful for the wise Christian mentors God has placed in our paths. The love of Jesus in our lives and in our hearts emanates to all those we come into contact with. It is the joy in our hearts to glorify Jesus and to help build the Kingdom of God. My husband and I are two very determined followers of Christ. The Holy Spirit has led me to start my very own women's ministry centered around helping empower women who are spiritually empty, lost, or wounded. Women who are stuck in the bondage of addiction, physical abuse, or any other hindrances to developing a closer intimate relationship with Jesus.

A Message to the Reader

IF YOU LIKED MY BOOK, WILL YOU CONSIDER SHARING ITS MESSAGE WITH OTHERS?

- Write a review on Amazon, Goodreads, or Barnes and Noble.
- Order a copy for someone who would be challenged or encouraged by it.
- Mention it in a Facebook post, Twitter update, Pinterest pin, etc.
- Invite me to speak to your group, church, or conference—it's my calling to share the message!